I0605080

LA REINA DE ESPADAS

TWO LINES
PRESS

THE QUEEN OF SWORDS

JAZMINA BARRERA

TRANSLATED FROM SPANISH BY

CHRISTINA MACSWEENEY

Originally published as: *La reina de espadas*

c/o Indent Literary Agency, www.indentagency.com

Two Lines Press
www.twolinespress.com

ISBN: 978-1-949641-87-5
Ebook ISBN: 978-1-949641-88-2

Design by Sloane | Samuel
Printed in the United States of America

Library of Congress Cataloging-in-Publication Data

Names: Barrera Velázquez, Jazmina, 1988- author. | MacSweeney, Christina, translator. Title: Queen of swords / Jazmina Barrera; translated from Spanish by Christina MacSweeney. Other titles: Reina de espadas. English. Description: San Francisco, CA : Two Lines Press, 2025. | "Originally published as: La reina de espadas"--Title page verso. | Includes bibliographical references.
Identifiers: LCCN 2024061787 (print) | LCCN 2024061788 (ebook) | ISBN 9781949641875 (paperback) | ISBN 9781949641882 (epub)
Subjects: LCSH: Garro, Elena. | Authors, Mexican--20th century--Biography. | LCGFT: Biographies.
Classification: LCC PQ7297.G3585 Z5513 2025 (print) | LCC PQ7297.G3585 (ebook) | DDC 863/.64 [B]--dc23/eng/20250531
LC record available at https://lccn.loc.gov/2024061787
LC ebook record available at https://lccn.loc.gov/2024061788

1 3 5 7 9 10 8 6 4 2

For Verónica Murguía

A dead person is a truth.

Elena Garro

A LIFE ON THE RUN

The beginning, at least, is clear. In 1916, in the small Asturian town of Cangas de Onís, a Mexican woman named Esperanza Navarro learned that her Spanish husband, José Antonio Garro, was having an affair with her cousin. Esperanza was eight months pregnant and understandably furious. So, she sold her jewels and set out with her two-year-old daughter, Devaki, for the port of Vigo. There, she boarded a ship bound for Veracruz, from where she took a train, with the intention of giving birth in Mexico City. Her body, however, had other plans and she went into labor in Puebla, where her sister Consuelo lived. On December 11, 1916, Elena Delfina Garro Navarro was born. And thus, while still in the womb, began a life on the run.

Elena Garro, la pérdida del reino (Elena Garro, the Loss of the Kingdom), p. 7.

A FIRST ENCOUNTER

At the beginning of 2016, I hadn't yet read Elena Garro's work. I was twenty-six and had read many other authors; I'd been studying literature and creative writing for at least six years, and was at that time working on a master's degree, so all I did was read. Garro's work hadn't been included in the curriculum of any of the schools I attended or the classes in Hispanic Literature I took during my English Literature major at the Universidad Nacional Autónoma de México. I'd been told that Elena Garro's plays were magnificent and from time to time had visited the bookstore in Coyoacán that bears her name, but I have to confess that, in 2016, I couldn't have come up with the title of a single one of her books.

The master's program where I was studying in New York required me to finish writing a novel: the story of a mother and daughter who fled from a powerful, violent husband and father. They were in hiding and feeling increasingly frightened of the world outside. Other things happened but that was the gist of the plot. I took my work in progress along to a number of workshops, where I received comments from my teachers and other students—such a wide variety of opinions was enough to make anyone crazy and the book began to resemble a Frankenstein's monster not even I could make sense of. One of the teachers, the writer Lina Meruane, tried to help me with that poor excuse for a novel, which still lies in its death throes in an old file on some hard drive somewhere. She advised me to read Elena Garro, specifically *Andamos huyendo, Lola* (We're On the Run, Lola) as it was similar to my novel. "Too similar," I remember her saying, and after that worrying comment I went immediately to the library to find the book. As I devoured those strangely beautiful, distressing stories, which did in fact have a lot in common with my novel—they were, of course, infinitely better but the similarities with what I wanted to write were there—I wondered just why it had taken me so long to find Elena Garro. Why was it so difficult to get ahold of her books in Mexico? Why was it that I eventually discovered her work in a foreign country, at the recommendation of a Chilean writer? Who on earth was Elena Garro?

RUNNING WILD

Esperanza Navarro's husband soon followed her to Mexico and the family settled in the capital. There is no other official record of Elena's early years. She recounts that she had a passion for the reverse side of things at that time; she used to explore the backs of pieces of embroidery, the undersides of furniture, and when she began reading, it was from right to left. In José Antonio Cordero's documentary *La cuarta casa* (The Fourth House), she says her father felt "very humiliated" by her tardiness in learning to read. But it was because she wasn't paying attention: "The nun would be reciting something like, '*amo, amas, ama,*' and I'd be looking at the specks of dust in the air." She thought that every speck of dust was a world where tiny people lived, and she made up stories about them. By learning to read back to front, she created a language of her own that only she and her sister Devaki understood and that the Teresian sisters who taught her considered heresy. She was made to stick a rose thorn into an image of the Sacred Heart as a sign of repentance. Elena wasn't repentant.

The family was living in Calle Guanajuato when her father's brother, Uncle Boni, his wife, Hebe, and their two daughters arrived from Spain. Soon, however, Hebe died and Boni fled the city in the throes of profound grief and despair. When José Antonio Garro eventually caught up with him in Iguala, Guerrero State, he moved his family there, and opened a store named Ciudad de México that had the exclusive right to sell the fabrics the Nahua people of the region commonly used in their clothing: *manta* and *cambaya*.

Elena Garro, la pérdida del reino, p. 9.

Elena would constantly return to those childhood years in Iguala, those "days of metamorphosis." In her memory, they are a space for freedom, for swimming in pools and climbing trees—one of those trees was called Troy and another Greece—and onto roofs to play with slingshots. Her parents, she recalls, were often occupied either working or reading: "They put us out in the garden and let us grow there like plants." While in Iguala, she was raised by Nahua women, absorbing their world view, hearing their stories and even witnessing the acts of violence perpetrated on them, particularly when the Cristero War spread to the area. She didn't go to school but read the Greek Classics and Spanish Golden Age authors with her father and uncle. She learned Latin and French, listened to the fairy tales her mother told her, wrote poems, and, with her siblings—Estrella and Albano had by then been added to the family—played at being Ulysses, Don Quixote, a king, a street vendor, or a Mexican general.

Cristales de tiempo (Time Crystals), p. 187.

La semana de colores (*The Week of Colors*), p. 125.

In the best text about her childhood, which she wrote for Emanuel Carballo in *Protagonistas de la*

Protagonistas, pp. 477-8.

literatura mexicana (Leading Figures in Mexican Literature), she says of her parents:

> They taught me imagination, multiple realities, love of animals, dance, music, orientalism, mysticism, a disdain for money, and military strategy by reading Julius Caesar and von Clausewitz. While I was living with them, I only ever cried for Christ and Socrates—the Sunday he drank hemlock—when my father read us Plato's *Dialogues*, which I've never reread.

"We learn everything in childhood," she would say years later, in an interview with Elena Poniatowska. And then she expanded on the topic: "Growing up involves gradually forgetting what we learned with such intensity"; "Those memories are what I most enjoy thinking of because, with the passage of time, all that is left is childhood; it's the only thing that seems real to me"; "Childhood is my constant point of reference. I experienced everything during that time, what followed has been just an added extra."

Diálogos con Elena Garro (Conversations with Elena Garro), p. 148.

In *Protagonistas*, she recounts frequent escapades: she and her sisters would escape into the hills, they threw their brother into the fountain to "watch him drown" and then did nothing until their dog rescued him, or one of them would hide in the water tank and the others would pretend she'd gotten lost.

Protagonistas, pp. 479-81.

Her sister Deva was sent to an elegant school in Mexico City and when her father asked Elena if she wanted to go there too or continue "running wild" in Iguala, the child replied, "I like being wild." Her father and other wealthy members of the Iguala community had set up a small school, and Elena was able to do whatever she pleased there, without fear of punishment. She'd climb onto the school roof, disguise herself with a bandana, sombrero, and dagger, and make raids on the homes of her extended family and neighbors. She was finally sent to Mexico City when she developed a penchant for arson and set fire to the house of a certain Carolina Cortina.

It was in Iguala that she first gave a public reading, when a school inspector ordered her to write a composition for Tree Day and, despite her protests, she was made to read it aloud.

FACTS AND CATS

What we conserve of the dead is, above all, images and words: in that, they are similar to books. We might even make the mistake of confusing the two, but no life fits in a single book. It would need several trunks, whole libraries, university and press archives to hold the vast, elusive life of Elena Garro, and what I write here doesn't aspire to that. It doesn't pretend to have the last word on anything or anybody. This isn't a biography, it's scarcely a notebook. It is a collection of stories, ideas, facts, and cats.

REAL ESTATE

The house where Elena Garro lived in Iguala was demolished and another—with a commemorative plaque—was built in its place. This house was put on the market in 2020. The white, three-story building stands opposite the Parish Church of San Francisco de Asis, by the Plaza de las Tres Garantías. The first floor consists of commercial spaces, including Foto Graciela, Nutri Jugos, and the Torre Fuerte bookstore, which sells romantic novels and offers two Bibles for the price of one. If I had the money, I'd buy that house tomorrow.

Memorias (Memories), p. 43.

CHILDHOOD

In one of her small, blue, spiral-bound notebooks, she copied the following words:

> "Le génie n'est que l'enfance retrouvée à volonté."
> ["Genius is no more than childhood recaptured at will."]
>
> Ch. Baudelaire

A WARNING

Elena Garro's best-known quotation is, "I am only memory and the memory that one has of me." The recollections we have of Elena Garro today are blurred and contradictory. This is something that perhaps happens with everyone after their death, but the process is a little more noticeable in her case because it's much harder to separate the facts from the lies, the lies from the literature, and the literature from the facts. The problem is that the verifiable events of her life are very often implausible. Added to which, Elena enjoyed inventing stories (or telling lies, you might say) about other lives and her own. And then the corrupt, repressive government she fought against in the mid-twentieth century, but with which she also attempted to ally herself, made it their task to distort history. And the events of her life frequently clashed with the interests of powerful men, capable of influencing official narratives. And she committed errors that anyone else would have tried to tone down or hide. And it was by no means uncommon for the men of her era—and some of those of our own, still—to discredit

Recollections of Things to Come, p. 3.

or even refute the testimonies of women, particularly when they dealt with claims of gender-related violence.

And so what happened was that I grew very fond of Elena Garro. This whole book should be taken with a grain of salt because, even though I never met her, I've fallen in love with her. I love her in those small parts of her scattered here and there, in her truths and her lies, because there is no space for indifference when faced with the huge personality of a woman who was brave, vain, charismatic, egocentric, brilliant: all that and so much more. I particularly love her for giving us *La semana de colores*, *Los recuerdos del porvenir* (*Recollections of Things to Come*), *Memorias de España 1937* (Memories of Spain 1937), *Un hogar sólido* (A Solid Home), and many other stories, some of the best that have been written about Mexico on its soil. About and from the soil. Stories that denounce violence against women, that describe the child's mind with astonishing levels of understanding, that speak openly of the perversity of the government, of racism, classism, and the struggles and resistance of indigenous peoples. Fantastical stories (even the most realistic) in which time is always the true protagonist.

SEVEN WOMEN

At the age of fifteen, Elena's father sent her to study in Mexico City. She graduated from the Escuela Nacional Preparatoria, where the student body at the time was made up of three thousand men and seven women. Elena lived in some luxury in the house of her aunt, Amalia Navarro, wife of the senator (and rumor has it, white-collar criminal) Lamberto Hernández. Along with her cousins, she attended ballet classes given by Hipóloto Sybine, who had studied with the legendary Russian dancer Anna Pavlova. Her cousin Amalia became a professional ballerina, choreographer, and founder of the Ballet Folklórico de México.

Elena Garro, La pérdida del reino, p. 11.

THE NAME

Elena Garro loved her first name: it is "so pretty," she says in a poem. She was named after Helena Blavatsky, the founder of the Theosophical Society, whose beliefs her father adhered to. Her middle name, Delfina, is an allusion to Delphyne, the she-dragon who guarded the oracle at Delphi, where the high priestess revealed truths and prophecies. In a number of texts, Elena used her middle name as a kind of pseudonym, and she also employed diminutives and short forms of Elena, such as Leli.

Elena Garro changed the spelling of her name depending on the circumstances; for instance, Octavio Paz writes in his letters that their relationship really began when she agreed to him calling her Helena. During their first months together, Paz wrote a love poem containing dozens of literary references to and etymologies of her name: "where, Helena, is your very name if we are only a little tenderness in the music?"

Odi et amo (I Hate and I Love), p. 46.

And in one letter he says, "the pronoun *mía* sounds very well beside your name. Just as does the *H*: the fact that you—and you alone among all the other

Elenas—have it, and that we use it as a sort of amorous code word, a sign of us, adds a new secret, ineffable bond to our—my—already bonded hearts."

Ibid., p. 89.

Years later, her lover Adolfo Bioy Casares would also refer to Elena as Helena in many of his letters to her.

Elena Garro and Octavio Paz named their only child Laura Elena Paz Garro, and during her life she was known and "written" as Elena, Helena, Helenita, La Chata, Chatita, and sometimes—by her father—Elynor. For a long time Elena Garro called her daughter Helenita and wrote her name that way to distinguish between them.

It's a common sexist practice to refer to men by their surnames and women by their first names, thereby excluding them from public life. I'm conscious of this, and yet I can't find it in me to call Elena Garro by her surname alone. It sounds cold, distant, and I already have an affectionate relationship with her ghost. So I call her Elena. And Octavio Paz is Paz because it's a lovely surname and I still retain a certain respectful distance in relation to him. To distinguish the daughter from the mother, I've decided to do the same as Elena: write the name of Helena Paz with an *H* and Elena Garro without. In spite of that decision, there are pages in this book that still sound like Elenic tongue twisters.

MARGINALIA

To reach the Firestone Library at Princeton University, you walk uphill along a paved path that runs between gardens with trees, flowers, and lime-green grass, ending in an open space surrounded by Gothic-Revival buildings. There's no way I can stop to look at them because I'm running late for an appointment with Cecilia at the entrance to the library, but I can't find either her or the entrance. I take a couple of turns around the quad, go up and down steps, until I finally discover the correct building. Cecilia sends me a message saying she's had to go to the archive and will wait for me there. The admission procedure is so complex that I'm slightly frightened: I have to call someone named Special Collections (that's how they sign their emails), go upstairs to be issued an identity card, then descend three floors to leave my things in a locker, taking with me only my computer and phone. Outside the archive, I have to wash my hands, give my personal information, wait to be admitted, follow the person from the counter to my assigned workspace, and say which of the boxes I'd previously selected I'm going to need that day. The *Elena Garro Papers* are well cared for; there's absolutely no doubt about that.

A box is brought to my table and I feel ridiculously moved to have before me papers that Elena Garro once held, to see the comical telegrams with their capital letters and terse phrases, envelopes with so many different addresses, religious pamphlets, and telephone bills. In the notebooks, I see her handwriting for the first time: doodles, phone numbers, stories, and book titles. The marginalia of an era and a lifetime. Slowly, careful not to damage anything with my clumsy fingers or misplace any document, I immerse myself in the *Elena Garro Papers.* I begin to familiarize myself with the personality of her handwriting, to distinguish her hurried script from the sad and from the consciously well written. For me, it is here—in their infra-ordinary minutiae, in the stains and crossings-out rather than the great secrets and confessions—that the extreme intimacy of these old papers resides.

THE FACE OF DANCE

Odi et amo, p. 40.

In 1936, she enrolled in the School of Philosophy and Literature at UNAM. In her first years there, she took classes in literature, Latin, English, and psychology and developed a passion for ballet and theater. Under the tutelage of Julio Bracho, she was an actress, ballet dancer, and choreographer. At the age of twenty, she worked with some of the greats of that time, appearing in a ballet based on André Gide's *Perséphone*, directed by Xavier Villaurrutia, and in Rodolfo Usigli's production of Molière's *The Bourgeois Gentleman.*

Recollections, p. 6.

When the protagonist of *Recollections of Things to Come* is dancing with her brother Nicolás, "a dazzled smile on her lips," people say, "Isabel! Who are you dancing for? You look like a crazy woman!" Elena wrote *Recollections* decades after giving up dance. And even later, while living in exile in New York, she dreamed one night that Dance appeared to her. "Don't you want to see the face of Dance?" it asked in her dream. And she said yes, she did, and she saw a smiling, red-haired man with black eyes, wearing a Pierrot costume.

Testimonios sobre Elena Garro (Testimony About Elena Garro), p. 352.

PROXIMITY TO THE STAGE

Elena adored the playwrights of the Spanish Golden Age. In an interview, she said she joined the theater group led by Julio Bracho because she wanted to be close to the "creators of fantasy" she understood best. She would have preferred to focus on acting rather than ballet but was convinced that her voice was too quiet. Her time in the worlds of theater and ballet, however, was short-lived. "The iron fist of an early marriage held me back from proximity to the stage." Decades later, during her exile in Spain and in dire financial straits, she was distanced from theater once again: this time she didn't even have enough money to join the audience. "Since I couldn't act in or watch plays, I decided to write them. But it isn't the same. No, it isn't the same." Elena wrote a total of sixteen plays, all of which were critically acclaimed. She became a benchmark, one of the most important figures in Mexican dramaturgy. In another interview, she said she found it easier to write plays than narrative fiction. It was the theatrical community that succeeded in bringing her back to Mexico in the 90s and that

Teatro completo (Complete Plays), p. xliii.

Ibid.

Ibid., p. xxxiv.

Elena Garro: Lectura múltiple de una personalidad compleja (Elena Garro: Multiple Readings of a Complex Character), p. 265.

organized tributes to her. One of these was a performance of her play *La mudanza* (The Move), during which Elena whispered to the cultural critic Patricia Vega that she was going to ask for a ban on performances of her plays; she really didn't like the staging.

Ibid., p. 128.

SNUBS AND COURTSHIP

In April 1935, during one of the many balls held in the Hernández Navarro house, Elena met Octavio Paz. She recounted the scene to Emanuel Carballo: Elena was with her cousin Pedro, "a Greek god," newly arrived from the United States and—she claimed—her "tragic, unspoken, overwhelming, enduring" first love. When Paz asked her to join him on the dance floor, she wasn't interested and told him she didn't dance. He replied, "I know your kind. You're a puritan and you've come here with the Protestant pastor of your parish." Elena and her cousin left the party and Pedro was only permitted to kiss her cheek once before his return to the United States.

Protagonistas, p. 484.

That snub was the beginning of a story of love and complicity, hatred and rivalry, a turbulent and volatile relationship that defies comprehension.

After that ball, Paz began to court Elena. She resisted his advances but at the same time gave him reasons to hope. She used to flirt with the other young men she preferred to him, but never let him completely off the leash. Paz, in turn, flirted with other women.

In her diary, Elena describes a number of tricky situations: for example, when two or three admirers turn up at her home at the same time. She notes:

Elena Garro Papers.

> My conscience isn't easy about poor Octavio. But at the same time, I don't want him to forget me. I don't want him to get used to being annoyed with me and so stop loving me. I might be an egoist, but not to that extent. I'd like to be able to really love him, or at least have the courage to tell him so—even if it's a lie—and be his girl. In the end, that should be enough; that they love you and you can respect them.

At one point it apparently was enough, but from that feigned love something more sincere gradually began to blossom.

Their courtship extended from June 1935 to May 1937. Paz wanted them to marry immediately but Elena's family—her parents eventually left Iguala and returned to Mexico City to live there with their children—and particularly her father were against the match and imposed a strict regime of supervised visits, under the threat of sending Elena to a convent. So the couple exchanged letters. Of that correspondence, only Paz's letters—in which love and passion are mythologized, abstract and metaphorical—are currently available to read. While almost always expressing himself in a prose embellished by his characteristic eloquence and poetry, Paz despairs at Elena's ambivalence and her resistance to physical contact and sexual relations. Elena was a Catholic in the 1930s, when the most common contraceptive practice—apart from infallible abstinence—was the far-from-reliable rhythm method. Sexual relations implied the real possibility of pregnancy and Elena wanted to continue her studies, to act and dance.

In 1937, Paz joined the International Brigades and moved to Mérida to teach in a school for the children of workers in the gum industry. From there, he continued to theorize his long-distance love in a way that was increasingly idealized, increasingly fantasized, but also increasingly threatened by his jealousy and Elena's rebellious spirit.

THE ELENIC GALAXY

One day, two years ago, I received a call from María Fernanda Álvarez with a proposal to write this book on Elena Garro. She was thinking of something quite short, nothing too detailed.

I don't consider myself to be impulsive, but on this occasion, I let my tongue run away with me. At the time, I'd read only two books by Elena Garro, both of which I'd found fascinating. I knew nothing of her life, was unaware that she had published seventeen titles—including a compilation of her theatrical works—had heard nothing of the messes she'd gotten into, and couldn't even have imagined just what I was getting myself into. So, I told María Fernanda that I'd be delighted, enchanted—more like bewitched, I now think—and I was happy to accept her proposal. I estimated a few months at most to complete my research and write that modest biographical essay. I thought that, in parallel, I'd be able to continue other projects already in progress or on my agenda. I was mistaken.

Two years later, I'm writing by a shelf that looks like an altar to Saint Elena Garro, to which I daily add such offerings as photos, post-it notes, to-do lists, and questions. Some months back, I made the decision to put my other projects on hold: I only write about Elena now. In my study, on the desk, are piles of new publications, books I've been given and those I've bought, those I've been wanting to read for a long time but haven't because I've spent two years reading her; her alone, and her readers, her disciples, her congregation, her family, her lovers, her friends, her detractors, her biographers, the hardened Pazians and the staunch Garrovians: an Elenic or Helenic galaxy of books I hate and books I love. This is still a modest biographical essay, but it's grown like one of those crossbreed dogs you adopt as a puppy, thinking it is going to be small, that turns out to be enormous and uncontrollable.

I often felt the urge to ask María Fernanda to allow me to change authors, to let me work on Josefina Vicens, for example, who wrote far fewer books, and made various movies that I could have watched from the comfort of my bed. A woman like Josefina Vicens would perhaps have been a better choice. And maybe María Fernanda would have given me permission, but "would have" and "could have" are unreal conditionals, and by the time it occurred to me to change authors, it didn't make sense: I was in it up to the eyes, totally dazzled by, irremediably lost in the universe of Elena Garro, in her labyrinthine multiverse.

GLOVES

The early courtship letters between Elena and Paz contain repeated references to a pair of her gloves that he keeps in his desk. They are a promise, a small anchor for an uneasy lover, a metaphor for touch, for the hand given in marriage, a fetish. He refuses to return them, says he has no intention of ever being separated from them, says that they are like having her hand and that he wants to marry her: "Will you be my wife? If you will, I'll be a genius, a good man." The gloves, he says, "obscess [sic]" him; the mere thought of them unsettles him and he becomes religious, with a form of Christianity that he will later slowly shrug off: "Pray for me to Jesus. Let Him enlighten us and be my balm."

Odi et amo, p. 76.

Ibid., p. 78.

Paz describes his fervor for the abovementioned accessories:

> I have your gloves. I carry them with me everywhere in my breast pocket, with your picture and my wallet. They are a token of you, a sign that you will return, not that you ever left. One

Ibid., p. 72.

> keeps a souvenir to make the absence more alive and the conviction of the irremediable more visible. Your gloves aren't a souvenir, they are a hope.

There's a photo from that time in which Elena and Paz are reclining together on a lawn, gazing into each other's eyes. Behind them are two palm trees that look like firecrackers. Paz has his left arm around her shoulder. Elena embraces him with her right arm and rests her left hand on his chest. She is wearing her black, chamois leather gloves. For me, this is the photo in which they look most truly in love.

YUCATÁN IMPERATIVES

Paz's letters from Mérida are as poetic as they are categorical, replete with advice and prohibitions. There is also an abundance of orders and reprimands. And the tone of these rises in parallel to his realization that Elena is an expert in turning a deaf ear to whatever he says.

He asks her to be "serious" and "austere," to send him the daily *El Nacional*, to stop working in movies "immediately," to answer his questions, to write smaller, to stop meeting Bracho and Usigli, her teachers, because he doesn't like them, to avoid going to bullfights, and to behave like "a well-brought-up child." He orders: "And while I'm on the subject, don't go out wearing pants." He finds the issue of pants particularly irritating and returns to it more than once. He also tries to persuade her to drop out of college; to give up drama, dance, and Socialist Youth meetings; to quit her whole social circle. The tone moves from the priestly advisor to a father scolding his five-year-old daughter:

Odi et amo, p. 334.

First: "It's idiotic, but put some order and method

Ibid., p. 211.

in your life, devote yourself to me, to yourself, to nurturing your inner being, so that your dreams aren't shattered, particularly not those most dear to me, those to do with your feminine perfection." "I don't want you appearing in the pages of *Hoy*, or getting involved in any other such frivolity. So, in that vanity fair, be serious and profound, as you were before."

And later, "I, your father, order you: under absolutely no circumstances, not for kisses or candies, should you leave your bed improperly dressed, nor should you dance; don't go out so often; take pills, heal yourself, and become a serious person, so deeply in love she's capable of sacrificing one evening to obtain a thousand." Ibid., p. 265.

He uses capitals for emphasis: "I INSTRUCTED YOU TO STAY HOME, but you continue going the Socialist Youth meetings, even though you know I don't want you going anywhere." "Don't go out so often. Think only of me," he orders. And the command I find most obnoxious is, "Stop being such a Piarist. Be a woman." By Piarist, he is referring to the religious order that founded the first free, public schools in Europe. That is to say, for Paz the feminine essence had nothing to do with study and knowledge. Ibid., pp. 339, 255, and 99.

He's furious when he discovers that Elena is continuing to accept roles in cinema, theater, and ballet productions: "This is unforgivable of your parents. Unforgiveable of everyone, of you. There are a thousand other occupations. But, naturally, dance, damned dance, and now movies. This is 'art'!! Isn't there any other job? And if not, isn't there poverty?" He advises Ibid., p. 335

her to leave behind all those temptations and suggests
Ibid., p. 210. she dedicate herself to adoring him: "Go deep into yourself, into the best of yourself, and you'll find a male image, not theater, cinema or cafés. Don't betray that image, that destiny; don't allow yourself to succumb to the weakest, falsest powers on Earth."

Ibid., p. 339. He orders her to retire from the world: "So, DON'T GO BACK TO ANYWHERE YOU DON'T NEED TO. The same goes for philosophy. You must be an enclosed nun, a child behind bars until I come back or you come to me."

DEATH IN PANTS

In the letters, there are at least eight death threats that can be considered rhetorical since we know that Paz didn't actually kill her.

> "That's how I am. Filled with great fury and love for you, my beautiful child, with the desire to have you and to kill you."

Odi et amo, p. 206.

> "You and all the other traitors will pay for this one day. I look at your portrait, your portrait, and don't know what to do, whether to love you or to kill you."

Ibid., p. 248.

> "I'm blinded with rage, and in that state, I send you this letter. I don't deserve what you've done, but you maybe don't deserve anything, not my rage, but perhaps a bullet, something that will annihilate you."

Ibid., p. 248.

> "I understand your situation. You don't understand mine. You must obey me automatically,

Ibid., p. 259.

without thinking, or I'll kill you. Don't be pig-headed."

Ibid., p. 252.

"Tell me if I should go on expecting your hatred. Are you ill? Well, die."

Ibid., p. 336.

"1. Give up the movies, the theater, all of it.
2. Don't go out anywhere. If you need a job, there are plenty that won't make me—and yourself—look ridiculous. If you don't stop, I'll kill you. The things you do are unforgivable. You've destroyed me. I'm lost for words."

Ibid., p. 205.

"I don't want letters in which you exist outside of me, I don't want you to live for anyone but me, because I've stopped time and your image, and I realize that I have that image alive here, close as a rose and thorn, as blood and bone, and I want you to stop time too and so kill me, and I want you to die."

Ibid., p. 341.

"A final recommendation: Never greet any of the subhumans you've had dealings with in cinema or its milieu: if I ever hear that you've so much as looked at any of them, I swear I'll kill whomever it was and put an end to everything. Rage: it won't let me live." (At least in this comment, the threat is not against her but everyone else.)

What was Elena's response? We don't know because we don't have her letters. Why didn't she break off the relationship? Was the notion of always obeying some older man so deeply entrenched in her mind? It's clear that she was often evasive, dodged the issue, lied, and then did exactly as she pleased. Paz would lose patience because however much he insisted, Elena went on doing the things she liked, with whomever she liked, and did it wearing pants.

So, just how much of Paz's character do these letters contain and how much is the dominant discourse and behavior of the 1930s? How far do they reflect what the average man did and said then, and how much are they the product of an individual's need to control, of a sense of insecurity, of superiority, of uncontrollable violence?

Elena referred to these letters in an interview:

> Whenever I went out, he'd write, "I beg you: a) don't do that; b) don't say that; c) don't go to that place..." You know, things like that, and when I read the letter I'd say, "Ay, I've done everything he told me not to!" And if any of the letters ever fell into his hands, Octavio would say, "They're loathsome, aren't they?" and I'd say, "Hombre, no, don't let it worry you, they're very informative."

Lectura múltiple, p. 139.

In the same letters, Paz told Elena about the feminist advances in the school in Mérida where he was teaching:

Odi et amo, p. 325.

From now on, we're all going to eat together. And one girl suggested we all wash the dishes. Some of the reactionaries were won over. Men and women undertaking the same tasks; the women will work in the fields too; the men will wash and iron like the women do. A new concept, a new consciousness is dawning, slowly.

Slowly!

RUMORS, RUMORS, RUMORS

I've spent months turning over every possible stone in an attempt to find Elena's letters to Paz. It's been worse than Genovevo de la O's siege of Jojutla, as my grandmother, and possibly Elena, used to say. And all I've come across are rumors, rumors, rumors. I've heard that the letters were still in existence at the time of Paz's death, but that his widow told some man that they would be published only over her dead body. Yet they weren't even published then because Marie José Tramini—the widow—died intestate. I was told that the Paz archive had been in very poor condition for a long time, there were fires and floods, but it was now being restored and might turn up somewhere, sooner or later. No one was able to say what became of the letters, if they survived jealousy, the climate, and institutional wrangles, if we'll ever be able to read them. It's just been announced that, out of respect for Marie José Tramini's wishes, the Paz archive will be available for consultation in 2043. I hate them all: Marie José Tramini, her wishes, and the people who decided to respect them. If I'm still alive and the letters are there, at the age of fifty-five, I promise to add a new chapter to this book.

A LETTER FROM 1936

There's a record of a single letter written by Elena to Paz in 1936. She writes at six in the morning, after a breakup that she considers "unpardonably definitive." In it she speaks of her disillusion, of how she used to think that "one day she'd be like that [in harmony with the infinite] with another being, immensely loved and loving, the two of us elevated so high that our hands would be touching the sky." She tells Paz that she tried to be faithful to God, to be chaste and, in spite of being with Octavio, write poems to God but she couldn't do it. Neither of them could do it. "It was enough for a pair of pants to appear before my eyes or a petticoat before yours for the sight of them to be more important than you or me." The conclusion she draws is, "we're complete failures."

Cristales de tiempo, p. 39.

FELIPE

In his earliest letters, Paz (Tavo or Tavucho, as he used to sign himself) tries to persuade Elena to "overcome" her inhibitions and consent to having sexual relations with him, using such phrases as: "There is a battle between your adolescence and the woman who throbs within you," or "abstinence is a return to adolescence." At a time when contraception was limited and pregnancy would have been the fairly inevitable outcome of a sexual relationship, their hypothetical child begins to appear in the letters as a recurrent fantasy and a means of chipping away at Elena's fears. Under the assumption that the child will be a boy, he is called Felipe, probably in allusion to a character on Goethe's *The Sorrows of Young Werther*. Paz calls him his "beloved impossible son," "our love eternalized," and says he could save them from "mundanity."

Odi et amo, p. 55.

Ibid., p. 107.

> Felipe is more than just a recompense for you or a compensation for me. He is a fruit. The children of love are very beautiful, you know. That's the reason for the beauty of bastards, who are

the product of loving emotions rather than social convention. Felipe will be the child of love, as joyful as love.

APPARITION

A few days ago, my deceased paternal great-grandfather, Alfredo Barrera Vásquez, appeared in Paz's letters to Elena. In 1937, while Paz was in Mérida, my great-grandfather was the director of the Museo Arqueológico e Histórico there and the two quickly became friends. They studied, worked, and visited archeological sites together. The past is a small world.

EPITHETS

During the courtship, Paz's letters transfigure, describe, and idealize his Elena with a thousand epithets. He calls her "sweet abyss," "sweet flower of life," "my dove," "my other half," "Asturian from Chihuahua," "the child with the most beautiful hair on earth," "my glory, my whole world," "Little Red Riding Hood," "insignificant blonde, divine little girl," "ignorant child," "insolent kid," "my goddess, Mexicana, my dream girl, my love, my hate, my conscience, my life," "water, tree, green, the color blue, my breath," "my homeland, my Mexico, Helena, the goddess formed of tears and semen," "adored one, bird tresses," "devilish, disobedient brat," "little Momma: you are my daughter and my friend."

Odi et amo, various pages.

In terms of her physical beauty, her grace and charm, her sensuality, for Paz there is something divine about Elena; she is a nature goddess, the archetype of the feminine taken straight from some Jungian handbook. In contrast, the epithets referring to her intelligence, humor, and self-determination ("disobedient," "insolent," "devilish") are rather comical and affectionately derogatory. Paz reproaches Elena for her use of irony, her humor, her intelligence, her critical distance; that is to say, her greatest literary tools.

Ibid., pp. 109, 127, 153, and 106

He pleads, "Don't put up defenses against your tenderness and love: you use irony and pain as a defense." He says that "intelligence is the deepest, most subtle form of unhappiness." He begs her to set aside "skepticism: that false, absurd form of wisdom." "Your irony, your terror of all things kitsch, your intelligence—a certain part of you—defended you from strange people, guarded your person, your amorous solitude, which was awaiting the moment to be given up," he explains (*mansplains*, we'd say now).

But as the years pass, Paz's letters gradually relax, become less solemn and melodramatic, more pleasant. If you were to ask me, I'd say he was learning humor from Elena.

THE AMBASSADORS

The Firestone Library at Princeton University has a huge number of archives related to Latin American writers. During that week various researchers were working there, plus me: a gatecrasher. We entered the archives at nine in the morning, went down to the basement, requested our boxes, immediately settled down to reading, transcribing, and absorbing as much as possible, and then left at four in the afternoon, dying of hunger and with headaches. On my first day, we gathered together outside the library to introduce ourselves. Who are you here for? someone asks. Alejandra Pizarnik, someone replies. And you? Virgilio Piñera, says a third person. There are also ambassadors for José Donoso, Sergio Pitol, and Juan Gelman. For my part—with my lack of methodology and the paleographic skills needed for dealing with manuscripts—I'm a lousy ambassador for Elena Garro. "Ambassadors?" says Cecilia—representing Donoso—"We're just professional gossipmongers."

SIGN HERE

According to Elena's version of events, on the morning of May 25, 1937, Paz appeared with a bunch of friends just as she was arriving to take a Latin exam and, without telling her where they were going, took her to the Civil Registry in Plaza Santo Domingo. Unaware of exactly what she was doing, perhaps unsure of how to resist or afraid of what might happen if she did, she married Octavio Paz. "When they ask what year you were born in, you say this," she claims Paz told her, because she was legally underage. Then she says, "The gentleman began reading a passage and I said it was really horrible." (It was the Epistle of Melchor Ocampo, which was used in such ceremonies at that time.) "And the man said, 'Stand up, you're getting married,' and he told me to sign here and here, and it was all over."

La cuarta casa.

Elena transforms the story of her wedding into something approaching an abduction. She is Europa and Paz is like Zeus in the form of a bull, luring her with false promises of the university (the symbol of education, study, and freedom). However, plans for the wedding were often mentioned in their correspondence and Paz's letters make it clear that not only did Elena know of these plans but she was also anxious to ensure they were carried through. And in order for the wedding to go ahead, they had to present a marriage license and undergo medical tests. It seems that there was even a celebratory dinner, organized by her sister Deva.

Odi et amo, p. 345.

Elena's version says that Paz falsified her date of birth and that her father was furious. Paz wanted to take her to his family home that very night, but Elena refused. When she continued to live in her own home for several more days, Paz officially accused her of desertion and so persuaded her to accompany him to his mother's house. On various occasions, Elena described the night when the marriage was finally consummated as a rape. In her *Memorias*, Helena Paz offers a narrative, based on what her mother told her:

Lectura múltiple, p. 318.

> He tore off her clothes and undressed too (my mother told me that for her it was a nightmarish scene and, innocent as she was, she thought my father had gone mad); he threw her on the bed, and as his penis wasn't hardening, he cursed and threw insults while furiously masturbating. My mother had very little idea of what was going on, then he slapped her hard a few times, punched her until she opened her legs, and entered her by force. My mother thought the pain would kill her. The sheet was soaked in blood; my father pulled it off the bed, opened the door, and called

Memorias, p. 45.

to his mother in triumph.

"Look! She really was a virgin."

Elena says that Paz's mother called her a "theatrical whore" and that they locked her in a room and refused to allow her to visit her parents. In a letter she wrote to Gabriela Mora, Elena escaped and returned to her family, at which point Paz threatened to have her father, José Garro, deported as he did not have Mexican citizenship. This persuaded her to return to him. But on her way, she stopped for a long time in a tram station, considering throwing herself onto the tracks. A night watchman who noticed how troubled she was accompanied her back to Paz's house and that murky episode, according to Elena, was the origin of her play *Parada San Ángel* (The San Ángel Stop), also called *Parada Empresa* (The Empresa Stop) in an earlier version.

Encounter with Memory; Elena Garro Tells Her Life to Rhina Toruño, pp. 35-8.

COFFEE WITH CREAM

As a child, Elena thought the only reason she'd ever marry was to be able to drink coffee with cream. "Because at home we were given oatmeal water instead. The only reason I ever found for getting married was to drink coffee with cream."

Protagonistas, p. 479.

"Although, to be honest," she says later, "I never thought about matrimony, nor did Deva. The world offered too many attractions to go shutting yourself away in someone else's house with a stranger. The very thought of it frightened us."

Ibid., p. 479.

MEMORIES OF SPAIN 1937

After the wedding, they traveled to the Yucatán with their friends Octavio Novaro and María Luisa Peñalosa. Then, in June, Elena gave up acting and dance and dropped out of college to accompany Paz to Spain, where he was to attend the *II Congreso Internacional de Escritores para la Defensa de la Cultura* (Second International Congress of Writers for the Defense of Culture). Years later, between 1978 and '79, Elena wrote a book, based on her diary entries for that trip, which was eventually published in 1992: *Memorias de España 1937*; one of her most endearing, charismatic books, an "anti-memoir," as Margo Glantz once termed it.

"I'd never heard of Karl Marx," is the opening sentence of the book, the story of a young university student who suddenly finds herself among a group of famous communist intellectuals in the middle of the Spanish Civil War. The flesh-and-blood Elena had in fact heard of Marx in 1937, probably without end: she'd attended meetings of the Socialist Youth, was a supporter of Trotsky, and had married a communist.

But in 1978, that is how the writer Elena begins to relate the adventures and mishaps of that young character, looking back from the future and giving free rein to her gloriously brilliant sense of humor.

The protagonist, the young, fictional Elena—whom the gentlemen of the left were given to describing as a lovely little bourgeoise, sometimes affectionate, sometimes impertinent—understands little of the political context of the war, the hounding of Anarchists and Trotskyites by Stalinist agents, the internal struggles between the various Republican factions, plus the tangle of other antagonistic elements of that pivotal moment in history. She puts her foot in it with almost every step: she comes close to death during bombings more than once, and a group of undercover Stalinist agents suddenly get it into their heads that she's a spy and almost arrest her. The character of Paz seems to be in a state of constant despair, scolding her and attempting to send her to her Spanish family so she'll stop being such a nuisance.

As all this is happening, Elena observes the intellectuals and draws amazing, moving, often comical portraits of some of the foremost personalities of the era. Rafael Alberti, Carlos Pellicer, José Mancisidor, Silvestre Revueltas, Juan de la Cabada, Fernando Gamboa, María Luisa Vera, Pablo Neruda, Antonio Machado, Miguel Hernández, Lupe Marín, Alejo Carpentier, Nicolás Guillén, María Zambrano, León Felipe, Luis Cernuda, Tina Modotti, and César Vallejo are some of the celebrities who file through a book that deals not only with, for example, Neruda's problem with earwax and Silvestre Revueltas's dipsomania, but also Vallejo's hunger and the mother of Antonio Machado, who, for Garro, embodies the metaphor of a Spain on the verge of collapse: "If one image of Spain stuck in my mind, it was that of Machado's mother, standing in that dining room with the flies buzzing around her."

Memorias de España 1937, location 1180 of 1629.

Elena speaks of the war and her affinity with communism, but also of her disillusion. She observes and also personally suffers hunger, destruction, and anguish: "No ideology justified such suffering," she says.

Ibid., loc 1113 of 1629.

In 1938, they returned to Mexico, where Elena's mother-in-law awaited her in their new home with a basket of socks to darn.

Elena Garro Papers, unpublished short story.

CONTRABAND

I'm flipping through a book of photographs of Octavio Paz and come across one from 1937, the year when he met my great-grandfather, Alfredo Barrera Vásquez, the father of my paternal grandfather. The photo was taken in Havana and in it, Elena Garro and Octavio Paz are having dinner with my other paternal great-grandparents, whose daughter, Isabel Bassols Batalla, was my grandmother. (When I later asked my father he remembered that the two couples were stopping off in Cuba on their way back from Spain.) That's when I realize that those great-grandparents had also attended the Congress of Antifascist Intellectuals. Narciso Bassols, my great-grandfather, was a diplomat and Clementina Batalla, my great-grandmother, was the second female law graduate in Mexico. There are certain similarities between Clementina's life and Elena's: both were brilliant, studious young women who set aside their professions for a long time when they married. My great-grandfather was a communist and it's said that he even counted my great-grandmother's chickpeas and made her give away her belongings. He also refused to allow her to practice her profession. When her husband died, Clementina returned to her law career and feminist militancy. She reminds me of Elena Garro because, among other things, at one point in their lives, they each traded contraband goods to make a living.

NUMEROLOGY

86 homes.
20 years married to Octavio Paz.
1 daughter (2 Elenas).
3 yellow tulips.
91 letters, over 13 telegrams, and 3 postcards
from Bioy Casares.
6 trunks.
1968.
20 years in exile.
17 books.
30+ cats.
14 yellow cardboard boxes.
A solid home.

TO THE HILT

In terms of the relationship between Elena and Paz, a famous female writer told me, "Best not get involved in that." I don't know if the writer in question was warning me off or giving me a piece of advice because she has a Mona-Lisa smile I can't read. With the unmistakable *tap-tap* of gossip, a friend told me that a female friend of his wrote a profile of Elena Garro and received threats for badmouthing Paz. Then his friend told me that wasn't true; nobody threatened her but I should still watch my step. Another friend told me that one of her male friends received threats for speaking ill of Paz, but then corrected herself to say it was Carlos Fuentes not Paz.

It seems that the paranoia Elena suffered from continues to follow her after her death. The intrigues are more like a game of Telephone than anything else, but it is a fact that passions blaze around those two figures, that a sense of danger, a taboo, surrounds them. I thought all this was funny until I found myself part of it, defending Elena Garro to the hilt, as though I knew her, as though it was a personal matter. Since then, I've been frightened too.

ISMS

Elena's ideological outlook not only changed with time but also depended on the character she was representing for the press, for writing, for herself. Her anti-communism was no secret. Although she was known to attend Socialist Youth meetings and was at one point a Trotsky sympathizer, she said it was a long time before she seriously studied Marx and that for decades her views were based on ignorance. The young Garro in *Memorias de España* asks if *The Communist Manifesto* is like Cervantes's "Speech on the Golden Age," and when she receives an affirmative answer, she replies that the comparison is enough for her to understand it.

After months spent amid intellectuals in Spain, the fictional protagonist opines that "the communists were right: some people were too rich and others too poor, and that was true of the communists themselves."

And of Marx's work, she says:

> I never read him or anything else Marxist until that damned attorney general Sánchez Vargas

> accused me of being "one of the leaders of the communist plot to overthrow the institutions of government." In 1970, I told Helenita Paz I was going to read *The Communist Manifesto.* Afterward, I realized that the term communist is applied very flippantly. What's more, the *Manifesto* is nothing like Cervantes's "Speech on the Golden Age." I decided to read all the Marxists, plus their forerunners, their contemporaries, their followers, and their opponents. I filled around 2,700 index cards and arranged them in files to be methodical. But it was too late...much later than I thought. I also discovered that the Marxists haven't read Marx or the other Marxists. There are so few of us who have taken that task seriously!

Memorias de España 1937, loc. 961 of 1629.

She hated Lenin but generally liked Trotsky, whose funeral she attended and whom she defended to other intellectuals: "I told them I was on Trotsky's side. María Izquierdo complained that I was amoral. Her Chilean husband, Uribe, and all the other drunkards sitting on the floor went on celebrating the murder." However, she did severely criticize Trotsky later, in the diaries she wrote in exile, when she spent a lot of time reading about the Russian Revolution.

Testimonios sobre Elena Garro, p. 154.

Her characters say things like creative artists cannot exist within communism, that established communism has justified mass murder, that monarchy is the only way to be transcendent because "kings and queens come to power in a state of innocence and are

Testimonios sobre Mariana (Testimonies about Mariana), p. 233.

accountable for us before the Church and God. Presidents arrive with blood on their hands, they enjoy a power that begins and ends with themselves. Unlimited power!"

Nor did she like contemporary capitalism, which she considered a despicable "fight between sharks over money."

Elena Garro, la pérdida del reino, p. 37.

When she became an ally of the reformist politician Carlos Madrazo, she said that if monarchy was not possible, she believed in democracy. She was a firm and constant believer in the Mexican Revolution and the redistribution of land, for which she fought beside the campesinos of Ahuatepec in Morelos State.

THE SMOKING HABIT

Memorias, p. 22.

Helena Paz said that Elena started smoking when she got married and went to live with her mother-in-law. She smoked menthols: two packs a day until the end of her life. A number of the mishaps she suffered in Spain in 1937 were related to her need to find tobacco during the wartime shortages. She used to sneak out behind Octavio Paz's back to buy cigarettes and then share them with the soldiers. That generous gesture gave rise to the suspicion that she was a spy and she was very nearly detained. She also shared her cigarettes with a group of German soldiers who were doing forced labor in the Basque town of Bidart during a vacation she took with her daughter in 1946. The locals disapproved of her friendship with the soldiers but she didn't care. One day, Helena—seven years old at the time—fell asleep on a dangerous section of the beach, which was cut off at high tide, and the soldiers swam out to rescue her. Those memories inspired a novella that is very dear to me: *Primer amor* (First Love).

José Bianco Papers.

In Paris, in 1948, Elena was diagnosed with a heart murmur and wrote, "Of course I have a heart murmur.

Probably thousands of them because I smoke like a chimney."

And in her exile diary, on June 4, 1978, she wrote in English (paranoia prevented her from writing in Spanish), "No money for cigarettes, for nothing."

Testimonios sobre Elena Garro, p. 442.

In many photos, she is pictured smoking while reading a book or newspaper (in one of her books she says she never reads the papers, but her diaries make it clear that she read them every day). In others, she's smoking while chatting to someone. In her later years, she suffered from pulmonary emphysema and a number of people remember her alternating drags on a cigarette with gulps of oxygen from a tank.

DIFFERENT PEOPLE

Laura Elena Paz Garro was born on December 12, 1939. Elena once said that seeing her daughter emerge with all her limbs intact was the happiest day of her life "because she was terrified the child would come out without any fingers or toes." The birth of Helena Paz and the choice of her name (despite officially being Laura, she was always known by versions of her middle name) initiated a life of the mirrors, the doubles, the foldings and unfoldings that is part of every experience of motherhood, although a little more so in this case. Helena Paz would be Elena Garro's companion for the rest of her mother's life and would share her grave afterward. It would be hard for Elena to imagine life before Helena. Their relationship deteriorated progressively throughout the years they lived together. Various people have said that by the end, when Elena Garro was an old woman and Helena Paz was addicted to barbiturates and alcohol, their arguments often escalated to the point where heavy objects were thrown at one another.

Lectura múltiple, p. 297.

There's one phrase that appears in several of Elena's

works: "Children are different people." In *Recollections of Things to Come*, Ana Moncada often says it, "astonished that her children were not herself." She repeats the phrase to convince herself that although they once lived inside her, *were* her, that is no longer true. This idea is reiterated in opposition to another one that also appears throughout her work: that of the double. For example, in the passage from *Testimonios sobre Mariana*, where she says, "That night, watching the mother and daughter, I had the strange feeling that the two of them were the same person and that one of them had invented the 'other' to make us believe she had a companion." On Sunday, June 22, 1980, while watching Helena sleep, Elena wrote the following lines:

Recollections, p. 26.

Testimonios sobre Mariana, p. 129.

She is my mirror,
I am her mirror
and nothing more exists
besides the hunger that circles
the rented furniture
within the four rented walls.

Cristales de tiempo, p. 216.

LOST WOMEN

In 1941, Elena started writing articles for the magazine *Así*, among which was a series of interviews with women: the actresses Lolita González Reachi and Isabela Corona, plus Frida Kahlo. She also wrote two pieces titled "Mujeres perdidas" I and II (Lost Women I and II) about a reformatory. For those articles, she had herself imprisoned and lived in the detention center for a number of days. On her release, she described the daily life there, the baths in ice-cold water, the gossip and intrigues, the punishments and tortures. Her accusations led to the director of the institution being fired.

El asesinato de Elena Garro (The Assassination of Elena Garro), pp. 65-8.

NO ROOM SERVICE

I'm staying in a cheap hotel (at least compared to the others in the area) on the outskirts of Princeton. "You should have gone to the priests, there's a diocesan house where they rent out rooms at reasonable prices," says Pitol's ambassador.

My hotel room is awful. There isn't a drop of light, it has dark drapes, like an opera curtain, and the only window looks out on the hideous parking lot below. But I came here to write about Elena Garro, who spent a large part of her life in hotel rooms, so I can't imagine a better place to be staying.

PEDOPHILIA

On their return from Spain, Elena and Paz moved for a time to Calle Saltillo 117 to stay with the Guerrero side of the family, while Helena Paz lived with her paternal grandmother.

Memorias, pp. 12-3.

One of Elena Garro's letters and a section of Helena Paz's *Memorias* relate a terrifying occurrence from that period. When Helenita was four, Octavio Paz's stepfather, José Delgado, raped her and infected her with gonorrhea. According to both the mother and daughter, Delgado had also raped a cousin of Paz, Mercedes Lozano. In a letter to Gabriela Mora, dated September 9, Elena says that a cousin of Octavio Paz by the name of Guillermo Haro y Paz confirmed the infection and the child was treated by the pediatrician Adrián Buckardt. Helena Paz recalls that the two families were together when Dr. Buckardt declared that she had been raped, and her grandfather, José Antonio Garro, ordered that no man was to leave the house before being tested for gonorrhea. At that point, José Delgado admitted that he had had the disease for years (he was unaware that there was a cure by then).

Sixty-five years later, Helena Paz still remembers the office where her genitals were cauterized with hot irons and says that, when she was cured, her father sent her back to live at her grandmother's house, where she was raped again.

DIARIES

Although there are many gaps in the collection, portions of Elena Garro's yearly diaries dating from her adolescence to her old age still exist: diaries written in small and large blue notebooks, diaries with certain pages ripped out, diaries that are neat copies, diaries that have seen better days, diaries left unfinished, complete diaries. The entry for June 25, 1976, is, "I had an argument with H. because she doesn't write her diary. I write unimportant things. I make notes just for the sake of it, and one day to tell the truth."

Testimonios sobre Elena Garro, p. 415.

HAUTE COUTURE

The family arrived in Berkeley in 1943. Octavio Paz had a Guggenheim Fellowship and then took on small academic and diplomatic jobs. Elena's sister Estrella was living with them because she was suffering from a form of TB that affected her eyes, and they didn't have enough money for her treatment. Elena worked as a maid in several homes in Berkeley because Paz wouldn't give her any money; he also refused to allow her to study at the university.

Memorias, p. 29.

After a while, Elena went to Mexico to sell contraband goods and look for a job.

Lectura múltiple, p. 320.

I think she maybe enjoyed picking out clothes in the United States and later selling them in Mexico. (Where? In the homes of her family and friends? I doubt if it was at market stalls. But you never know.)

Elena loved clothes. She's described as buying very expensive outfits by Chanel and Dior, plus panther fur and antelope skin coats. She said designers let her have clothes because she looked so good in them, that Cristian Dior wanted to employ her as a model (in her *Memorias*, Helena Paz recalls the day Dior came to

Memorias, p. 138.

visit her mother at home and said, "She is so beautiful, exactly the sort I need") but Paz "kicked up a terrible fuss." Even years later, when they were living in poverty, she and her daughter spent most of their small income on luxurious clothing.

Lecturas múltiple, p. 322.

In photographs she appears to be conscious of her image, of her long legs and slender figure. A number of her protagonists are physically like her and the narratives tend to stress their beauty, although Elena herself could often seem modest in her dealings with others. When Emanuel Carballo reproaches her for basing the character of Mariana on herself and making her too good-looking, Elena responds, "Naturally, I wanted to give her a touch of glamor (remember that I'm a petit bourgeoise). I couldn't make her as plain as the author because then the whole plot of Mariana would go downhill. Anything is permissible in literature."

Protagonistas, p. 496.

THE LOST GOOSE

In his letters from Berkeley, while Elena was in Mexico, Paz is much more affectionate, amusing, and irreverent. "The thing is that without you, without our child, I feel like I'm in a foreign atmosphere, like a fish out of water, a savage in the city," he tells them. He's also much less deeply in love. He ended up taking responsibility for Estrella's care while she was in the sanatorium; his letters give Elena detailed accounts of the state of her sister's health and her spirits and speak of his attempts to bring a smile to her face. He also writes letters addressed to the two Elenas, telling them about the fog in San Francisco, a neighbor's lost goose, and his boring work. He writes in purposely lousy English to make them laugh.

Odi et amo, p. 76.

Paz comes across as being resigned, irritated, and unwilling to address their relationship. He writes that he'd prefer to talk about money, and often does: about bills, his debts, about "business":

> But all that is in the past and I don't want to go back there, much less in a letter that is, unavoidably, about business because business is

Ibid., p. 426.

> the only real thing, the only thing that doesn't hurt, and the only thing that has a beginning and, thank God, an end. What we have has no beginning or end. It's more like a mood than a situation. We could talk till kingdom come without ever managing to straighten anything out.

The letters are also less imperative. Paz claims he's glad Elena is working, that things are going well for her, that she's going out and is happy. For his part, he's involved in affairs that he doesn't mention to Elena, but he hints that he wouldn't mind if she were to do the same. Elena is deeply offended by that, and in her diary recounts that when she read the letter, she launched a jar of extremely expensive cream at the mirror. The offending letter says:

Ibid., p. 415.

> It seems to me impossible that nobody has fallen in love with you, and there's no point in kidding each other; isn't the plot [of a screenplay he asked Elena to show to people in the film industry] a lover's game? Aren't you there with the Argentinian [he doesn't say which Argentinian man, but it isn't Bioy Casares or José Bianco, whom she met later], the psychiatrist, etc.? It's not your fault you're adorable or a long way from me; nor are you completely at fault for never having been happy with me.

In another letter, he suggests they separate:

> It would be less painful if you were to tell me that you'd fallen in love with someone because what pains me is when you say you feel you've been shipwrecked without even a straw to grasp at. I don't know if what I have for you—and the child, who is now daily at the forefront of my mind—is love. You are the only beings who keep me awake at night and cause me anguish… Maybe there's no remedy; maybe a separation would be for the best.

Ibid., p. 417.

Who knows if he loves her less or is still in love with her, but the truth is that he treats her better and even supports her in her work and her professional career.

> In general, I feel you've found your path in life: you seem enthusiastic, furious, and happy, loving your work and with a different vision of things. That's what I wanted, what I've always wanted for you: to put your talent, charm, and abilities to good use and not to destroying yourself, to destruction… And don't give up on your career for anything in this world; you'll go far.

Ibid., p. 426.

WRITING TECHNIQUE

It was most likely in her childhood, when she was studying with the Teresian Sisters, at the same time as she developed an interest in the reverse side of fabrics, that Elena learned to embroider:

Protagonistas, p. 483.

> When she [her aunt] was going out for a walk, to prevent me from wreaking havoc, she'd order me to 'embroider four roses' on the tablecloth I was making in the handicrafts class. I was good at embroidery, but four was a lot of roses and left me no time for playing marbles or using my slingshot. I taught my cousin Poncho to embroider and between us we could get through the task more quickly.

Diálogos con Elena Garro, p. 271.

Her love of textiles and embroidery was linked to her writing technique. In an interview with Roberto Páramo, she says, "My technique for writing is sewing; whenever I sit down to write something, I start to embroider. Each stitch I make is like writing a word, and as I follow the pattern, the garland or daisy, I'm constructing the plot, a scene, or situation." "If I didn't embroider," she continues, "I couldn't write."

Many of the characters in her works embroider. In *Recollections of Things to Come*, for example, Ana Moncada is seen on several occasions with a needle and embroidery frame. When she says that she's longing for "a good earthquake," she jabs her needle angrily into the piece of embroidery she's holding. In the 1940s, Elena wrote in her diary that Octavio Paz wouldn't let her sew: "I'm not supposed to embroider. He's forbidden it. When he comes in, I hide my hoop and the cloth."

Recollections, p. 31.

Testimonios sobre Elena Garro, p. 168.

Where did I read that Elena had embroidered the drapes in one of her homes?

DREAMING IN ANOTHER'S HEAD

I've dreamed of Elena Garro a number of times and almost all those dreams have left me with brief, inconclusive pictures: a blurred image of Elena standing up, wearing a coffee-colored, tailored suit; Elena Garro and Bioy Casares laughing at something awful, with Octavio Paz looking worried. I once dreamed that Elena entered a worm spiral of time and space that carried her from Los Angeles to San Francisco. Another night, I dreamed that Elena and Helenita were Lorelai and Rory from the television series *Gilmore Girls*.

I adore the play Elena wrote called Benito Fernández, about a market stall selling heads. You can take off your own and put on one belonging to a dead person. The heads come with everything intact, memory and all, and there's one, belonging to the young Ulloa, who used to dream a great deal "of ponds, lakes, violins, sailboats, and even swans." Each of her dreams becomes a hair and when the purchaser puts on the head, they can inhabit the dreams. "Don't you want to get to know the dreams of the dead?" the stall owner asks a potential customer. "They're real dreams and

Teatro completo, p. 247.

will help you understand your own," he insists.

If only there were a stall like that in La Lagunilla Market, where they had the head of Elena Garro. Not to buy, but to rent for a time. Just a short time, because a head like that would be heavy, would immediately give you a stiff neck, a migraine, and goodness knows what else. I'd only be able to stand it for a few minutes, a couple of hours at most, but I really would like to rent it, with everything intact, and her blonde locks of dreams and nightmares. "My dreams give me advice and though the family didn't believe it, they always came true," says the protagonist of the play *Sócrates y los gatos* (Socrates and the Cats).

Ibid., p. 308.

FRAGMENTS FROM NEW YORK

After staying a while in Mexico, Elena wanted to return to San Francisco but (she says in her diary) Paz asked her not to because they couldn't afford it.

In 1945, she went to work in New York (against Paz's will, according to the diary) to earn enough to continue paying the bills of her sister, who was hospitalized for seven years. She found a job as an editor at the Spanish-language magazine *Hemisferio*, published by the American Jewish Committee, and lived in the Santa Lucía Hotel on Bank Street with a woman named Ana Carner. During that time, Octavio Paz was teaching at Middlebury College in Vermont and was having an affair with the Chilean translator Carmen Figueroa.

Elena had to leave her job in New York because Paz and Ramón Araquistáin—a friend of Paz and Elena's lover, who was known as Finki—insisted that she move to Vermont. But she was hardly in the door before Paz kicked her out, and she had to return to New York, with only seven dollars in her purse, and beg for her job back. Then Paz came to New York but lived apart from Elena.

Tensions ran high between the couple because Paz didn't want his daughter, who was still in Mexico, to join them in New York. After a "violent dispute," Paz finally agreed to let Helena Paz come to New York. The fragments that remain of Elena's diaries from that period say, "Octavio won't divorce me. He burst out laughing… 'You're trying to make me jealous'… 'I'm pregnant'… I'm looking for somebody to do the abortion… I don't want it. Finki is repulsive."

Testimonios sobre Elena Garro, p. 157.

Ibid.

In *Memorias*, Helena says that Finki had been a very tender lover to her mother, but when she told him she was pregnant he said, "Listen, you're not going to tie me down with that; I'm not interested in being loaded with that package. Let's see how you manage to get it out of your belly."

Memorias, p. 46.

Her discontent grows in each of the following diary entries: "I thought the anguish was driving me mad… I'll go on working for that Jewish paper for a miserable wage. Who will take care of the child? The idea of going back to Paz is terrifying." But in the end, they get back together and Elena and her daughter go to Paris with him.

FEMINISM OR SOMETHING LIKE THAT

Lectura múltiple, p. 51.

Elena didn't consider herself to be a feminist: "Just as soon as we have ideas of our own, I'll be a feminist, but while we're still using a masculine intellect, I'm not," she said to Verónica Beucker in an interview, although in similar situations she uses the word "feminist" more informally. For instance, when speaking to Reynol Pérez Vázquez in 1994, she says that Christ was a feminist because first he allowed himself to be seen by women and later he protected and sheltered Mary Magdalene.

Ibid., p. 201.

Diálogos con Elena Garro, p. 961.

As the queen of paradoxes, despite having had more than one abortion, she said that she wasn't in favor of the practice because she thought the fetus had rights too.

In terms of theory, it's clear that Elena's reasoning doesn't have its origins in feminism. However, her work is filled with denunciations of violence against women, protests, and criticism of male abuse. There's an intuition in her works, a perspective that I can only call *feminist.*

A number of her books highlight physical violence perpetrated on women. The best examples of this are perhaps in her plays *Los perros* (The Dogs) and

El rastro (The Trail). *Los perros* deals with the cyclical and systematic rape of the women in a family: "Then he bought a pistol and hit me with it, and, when I was bathed in blood, he took me. That's how my mother found me! Seven long years her search lasted as nobody would tell her of my whereabouts." The magnitude of the physical abuse in this story is so great that the women's only option is heartrending resignation: "We don't cry, we just look on while unhappy thoughts come and go. Such is the lot of women in this land of God!"

Teatro completo, p. 174.

Ibid., p. 175.

El rastro narrates the femicide of a pregnant woman and the apprenticeship of violence, a curse that is passed from generation to generation. "They close their eyes so as not to see the unhappy lot of Adrián Barajas, seated here, just like his father, who stuck thorns in the back of her knees and made his mother drink her own blood." There is no censure in the play; the crudeness of the violence is devastatingly explicit.

Ibid., p. 271.

In other books she protests against censorship and women's lack of freedom of expression:

> She remembered her father and grandfather speaking about how unbearable women were because they talked so much… 'Shhh! Be still, remember that a closed mouth gathers no flies!' And Conchita remained on this side of the phrase, alone and stupid, while her grandfather and her father went on talking for endless hours about the inferiority of women.

Recollections, p. 169.

She repeatedly criticizes the stereotypes that discredit women's intelligence. For instance, in *Sócrates y los gatos*, the protagonist's father says to her: "What a shame you're intelligent! It pains me so much I could cry from here to eternity. Women should be stupid... Haven't I told you that? No. I'm always forgetting to tell you to be stupid..."

Teatro completa, p. 336.

The notion that the institution of marriage deprives women of their identity also appears in several passages. In *Recollections of Things to Come*, Isabel muses that "the idea that a woman's only future was matrimony [was] humiliating. For them [her family] to speak of marriage as a solution made her feel like a commodity that had to be sold at any price."

Recollections, p. 17.

When being interviewed by Rafael Luviano and Ricardo Pacheco, Elena says that women are traitors because "we have to accept the ideas or the rule of an overlord," and she then explains the importance she lays on the will to shatter oppressive structures: "True, women have lived under subjection but to a great extent that depends on the woman because nobody can subject you if you don't want it. I'm very independent, you have to go whole hog. But if you stop to think, the cost is high."

Diálogos con Elena Garro, p. 961.

In terms of writing by women, in a letter to Gabriela Mora, Elena tells of how she was invited to a conference to talk about "feminine literature" and offered the following opinion: "It's not bad, is it? You could say that when a woman writes, she dies. It's her death sentence."

Lectura múltiple, p. 332.

NOSTALGIA FOR CATASTROPHES

The concept of "nostalgia for catastrophes" appears in her work at least twice. She is perhaps referring to the anguish of the calm before the storm, the suffering of passive aggression and cold wars—both military and personal—being worse than overt explosions. But it could also have to do with a sort of Stockholm syndrome or masochism, or simple boredom. For which of the various catastrophes Elena endured did she feel nostalgia?

THE EYES OF ANIMALS

The hotel in Princeton has no redeeming features, but behind it is woodland with trees I can't quite identify, something like satin walnut or maple. All green. This evening, I went out for a walk. There was still a little light in the hotel parking lot, but farther on, in the woods, the shadows of the trees were hurrying along the night. Fireflies were twinkling all around, and just a few yards away was a stream where a magnificent deer was drinking. I stood stock still to avoid frightening it and she (I now think it was a doe because it had no antlers, and because that's what I want to believe) went on drinking. Very slowly, I moved closer, but the animal immediately heard my footsteps and froze, watching me watching her. We both stood like that for a few seconds, until she ran off. I like to imagine that doe was Elena Garro. "The heavens that await me are in the eyes of animals," says a character in her play *Parada San Ángel.*

Teatro completo, p. 390.

BLUEBEARD

When Elena G. and Elena P. left for Paris in 1946, in her diary, Elena G. wrote: "A dramatic farewell from Mama. Chata cried the whole evening and night. Anita helped to pack our trunks. Octavio has asked for sheets, soap, chocolate, coffee, cigarettes, sugar, everything." *Testimonios sobre Elena Garro*, p. 157.

On the deck of the ship, a man named Jiri Kallab saw her crying and asked, "Is your boyfriend staying behind in New York?" Elena said no. "Your husband?" Ibid. "No. It's the other way around. My husband is in Paris and I'm going to meet him there," she explained and went on crying.

Octavio invited Finki to live with them in Paris. She despised him: "Finki insists that he's in love with Ibid., p. 158. me. I pity him. Poor thing… Does he think I'll forgive him for the pregnancy?"

In Paris, they lived at 199 Avenue Victor Hugo. There, the following year, she met the Argentinian author José Bianco, who followed her everywhere, called her, and sent gifts. In her diary, Elena wrote Ibid., p. 163. that she'd had enough and was doing her best to avoid him. She left Paris for a vacation and asked Paz not to tell Pepe Bianco where she was going, but Paz ignored her request and told Pepe, who then set off after her. Elena had to change her ticket to escape him.

When she returned from Italy, Finki and Bianco were still hanging around her. The situation with Paz was awful. Elena complained that he moaned the

Ibid., p. 165.

whole time about not being a better writer. "What an ego!" she wrote. "I'm decided; I can't get a divorce: I don't have a cent and, what's more, Octavio would get custody of Chata."

Then she attempted to commit suicide. She turned on the gas, gave Helena three sleeping pills, took another three herself, and lay down next to her daughter.

Ibid.

When Helena Paz woke up, Elena told her to go back to sleep. Narciso, the Spanish cook who worked in the house, found them and woke them with warm salted water; he opened the windows and sent news to Paz, who arrived that night with Finki. They were both furious, said that Elena should be locked away in an asylum; Paz called her a murderer.

Memorias, p. 104.

In *Memorias*, Helena says that not long afterward, María Zambrano, who was staying with them for a while, discovered Elena in the dining room, lights out, hanging with a lamp cord around her the neck. She asked Teodora—a woman who worked in the house—and Finki for help, and together they took her down and laid her on the dining table. They managed to bring her around and then gave first aid, so saving her life. Paz wanted her to be taken to a "lunatic asylum" but María Zambrano "roundly refused to let him," and as Paz had great respect for her, he gave way.

"Don't they know that all I want is never to hear them again?" Elena wrote in her diary.

Testimonios sobre Elena Garro, p. 165.

After that episode, Paz began to keep a close watch on her and restrict her movements: "Octavio never buys me anything. He pays the weekly costs of Narciso, the gas… Octavio prefers me not to touch money. And I don't." She seemed resigned, said that she was a terrible housewife.

Lectura múltiple, p. 168.

She had a drawer where she kept her letters from Finki and the other men who wrote to her. Paz used to say that it was like Bluebeard's chest and demanded the key. She wouldn't give it to him.

In her diary and letters, boredom becomes a recurrent theme. In 1948, she wrote to her father, "I have nothing to tell you about Paris, it's the same cold weather, the same fog, the same 'chic.'" She described it as "a very boring city, not easy to live in." She was thirty-one and said her spirits were extremely low; she was leading a monotonous life, where everything was "always the same"; Paris was "as cute as ever and as boring as ever too." She wanted to isolate herself and enjoy her solitary bicycle rides.

Elena Garro Papers.

José Bianco Papers.

In the meantime, Paz's agenda was filled with male friends and visitors. "He goes out for walks with them like a leading lady with a bear," Elena said.

Ibid.

In August of that year, Elena and Paz took a vacation alone and the marriage underwent a brief, unexpected return to closeness. "Octavio experienced a kind of sicura [sicura can refer to either a Chilean shepherd's pipe or a dance]…he turned into a charming boy… Venice made us forget ourselves, forget we were married," she

Ibid.

wrote in a letter. But that harmony was short lived, the arguments and the lovers soon returned. Elena briefly toyed with the idea of shacking up with a Roman: "I spent a few weekends there, the boy is very handsome and eloquent, but the idea of sleeping with him and having children was quite repellent." So she returned to Paris: "I promised to go back and file for divorce. I haven't done anything about it yet." And she resigned herself to the tedium. "The only thing that changes is the child, who is growing day by day and becoming a sweet, peaceful Chata. Paris is just the same, but with more cars, better bread, and more Mexicans." Elena and Paz then had such a serious argument that she moved out and didn't return until March 1949.

Ibid.

Lectura múltiple, p. 332.

José Bianco Papers.

The truth is that, despite the drawbacks she describes, Elena's social circle began to expand. She struck up friendships with André Breton, the poet Benjamin Péret, Pablo Picasso, Jean-Paul Sartre, Albert Camus, and various other artists and thinkers. The influence of the Surrealists on her work was particularly strong in a number of her plays.

Testimonios sobre Elena Garro, p. 169.

She would sometimes invite *clochards*—vagrants, one of whom was also named Elena—home to wash and have a meal, much to Paz's chagrin. She also helped the painter Francis Picabia, who was living in dire poverty at that time. María Zambrano used to send beggars to her for help.

Ibid., p. 170.

When Bianco returned to Buenos Aires, Elena began a frequent, close epistolary friendship with him. In her diary, she says that she's going to miss him, even if he was a very time-consuming snob.

SPECTERS IN THE WINDOW

In the archive, I request Series 3: *Correspondence of Elena Garro, 1935–1998*. I ask for boxes seven, eight, and nine, which contain letters to Elena Garro from Bioy Casares and Octavio Paz, two of the most important men in the story of her life.

A friend of mine told me that he'd been in this very same room and, having known Paz personally, had felt dreadfully ashamed to be holding this correspondence in his hands. It was as if he were violating something secret, intruding into the private lives of those people, those dead people. Now, as I read through the letters, I too feel like an intruder. The past contained in these pages is so alive that I suddenly have the sensation that I am the specter, a spirit spying on that passionate dialogue. But for me, neither shame nor modesty is the predominant emotion; I'm curious, have shivers running down my spine. It's like the excitement of reaching the denouement of a telenovela. During this whole period of research, I've never understood why Elena, who was unhappy with Paz, didn't leave him for Bioy, who—it has to be said—seems to have been a pretty likeable sort of man. A Don Juan, of course, but at least handsome, charming, and affectionate.

The paper of Bioy's letters is almost transparent, as thin as the peel of new potatoes, like onion skin or insect wings, like those strips used for bad breath and the drugs my ex used to take.

I read frantically, although stumbling many times over Bioy's ridiculously difficult handwriting. It looks lovely but is incomprehensible.

And as I read, I have that sensation given by the literature I like best: looking out a window and suddenly seeing, like a ghost, my own reflection on the glass.

A window into other minds, into love and pain seen by other eyes, in other times. And a reflection, because that's how we humans are: alike. Once, for example, I was in love with a married man, and it's a memory I've disdained for years, set aside because I repent my feelings, because it was a humiliating relationship that took me to a place of fear, uncertainty, and loneliness. But as I read those letters, I also remember how powerful that desire was, and how, being unrealizable, it never waned. That almost imaginary bond that allowed me to idealize to my heart's content, to write letters, to fantasize (create pipe dreams of) improbable lives, to build castles in the air.

The letters contain useful information; they clarify many things but don't solve the mystery, just make it more mysterious.

TELEGRAMS

In 1949, on the recommendation of her friend Pepe Bianco, Elena met Bioy Casares and his wife, Silvina Ocampo, in Paris. She wrote in her diary that day, "Meeting with the Bioys at the George V. Strong impression. We're going to have dinner later at the Rhumerie Martiniquaise. A fortune teller predicts that Bioy and I will have a grand amour."

Testimonios sobre Elena Garro, p. 186.

His prediction turned out to be accurate. For Elena, Bioy was "the craziest love of my life, which is almost killing me."

Protagonistas, p. 483.

Elena was not, by a long shot, Bioy Casares's first lover. Even on that trip when they met, Bioy and Silvina Ocampo were accompanied by a niece of the latter, who was, like many others, the charming Bioy's lover. But he never established as close a relationship with other lovers as he did with Elena.

Bioy's concise telegrams offer a good synopsis of the general tone of his love letters:

1950
LONGING FOR NEXT MEETING IN PARIS

Elena Garro Papers.

LOVE AND MISS YOU
BIOY

1951
THE LONELY FOOL DEEP IN LOVE MISSING YOU
BIOY

UNDATED
DEVASTATED WITH MISSING YOU LONGING FOR YOU
BIOY

1951
MISSING YOU LOVING YOU SO MUCH DON'T KNOW WHAT TO DO WITH MYSELF
ADOLFO

UNDATED
WISHING YOU HAPPINESS LOVING YOU
BIOY

JANUARY 26 1955
WOULD LIKE YOU TO COME TO OUR HOUSE IN MAR DE PLATA STAYING THERE FEBRUARY MARCH
LOVING AND MISSING YOU
BIOY

SEPTEMBER 1955
SENDING AIRMAIL STORIES PROLOGUE

EMBRACE ULYSSES I MISS YOU WAIT FOR YOU LOVE BIOY

1957
LONGING FOR NEWS
BIOY

1959
TWENTY-SEVEN NEW YORK STOP NUMBER OF ADDRESS 1650
BIOY

I'm leaving this one for last; it seems to me the funniest and most enigmatic of all.

1956
MY FATHER PASSING THROUGH TONIGHT IN ARGENTINIAN MILITARY PLANE TRY TO GIVE HIM NEWS WAITING
BIOY

Desire features strongly in his letters. The desire, for example, to "hold your hand, or one of your feet, in mine." And there is also stoicism: "I must resign my- Ibid.
self to conjugating the verb *love*, to repeating for the thousandth time that I never wanted anyone the way I want you, that I admire you, respect you, like you, that you make me laugh, excite me, that I adore you." They are filled with declarations: "I love you more than anyone, including the dog." With eroticism: "And then, then, our lovemaking; I've never made

love with anyone the way I have with you and I'll never forget those evenings—we really had traveled to distant lands—of joyous abandon." What isn't remembrance is the future, speculation about what they will do and see together. Bioy sends letters from Italy, Buenos Aires, Montevideo, and France. There's no lack of empty promises, the clichés of stories of adultery, "Wait for me," "I'll be back before you know it."

In the correspondence, Bioy often describes himself as an enamored ghost. "This ghost is still in love," he says, and speaks of his "inconsequential life as a carefree ghost." He signs off, "this ghostly Bioy," with the hope that "my letters won't be ghosts." "It's strange," he writes, "this state of living with your mind in one place and your soul in another. There's no doubt that it must be an apprenticeship for ghosthood.... What a pain to be representing romanticism a hundred years too late." And, "I'm like the ghost of a repentant suicide." As she invents the plot of her novel *Testimonios sobre Mariana*, Elena recreates and remembers that romance, its comings and goings, its sublimation, impossibility, and incomprehension. *Testimonios* is, among other things, a novel about the ghosts of repentant suicides.

Bioy also encourages her to write. For instance, in 1950, he says, "You should write. That writers have bored you is a fortuitous circumstance in your life and only has importance for you; your writing is important for everyone." On several occasions, he invites her to collaborate with him (possibly more like work for him), to translate him into French, adapt his novels for the screen, and be his literary agent in France.

TURN OF THE SCREW

I didn't enjoy *Testimonios sobre Mariana.* I found Mariana, the protagonist, boring; she had me tearing my hair out and even though I knew that she wasn't Elena Garro, I recognized so much of the author's life in her that she turned me off of the actual Elena Garro. Both of them such attention seekers, such martyrs. Such a desire to be and play the victim, to allow oneself to be trampled underfoot, to suffer, suffer, and go on suffering. But I liked the ending, that fantastic turn of the screw that gives new meaning to a large part of the story. And then time passes, and I often find myself thinking of *Testimonios sobre Mariana.* More and more passages return to me, and I'm not sure how it happened, but it now seems like a magnificent novel.

PHANTOM ARCHIVE

The issue of the letters from Elena Garro to Bioy Casares is also an enigma. In Argentina, I'm told that nobody knows where they are, that Bioy Casares's archive isn't accessible and there's a mystery surrounding the identity of the custodians. I make phone calls that nobody answers, send letters nobody replies to; I can't even dig up any gossip.

A GAME OF QUESTIONS

In Elena's diaries there are a number of Surrealist exercises that she called "the game of questions," which consisted of writing a question on a piece of paper and folding it over. Then someone else had to answer the question blind, without seeing it. What follows is an example written by Octavio Paz, Elena Garro (who writes her name with a H here), Helena Paz (called La Chatita in the game), Carlos Fuentes, Archibaldo Burns, and two other guests, Lucinda and Portilla:

Testimonios sobre Elena Garro, p. 216.

> Octavio: What is Sunday?
> Helena: It's the imprisoned unicorn.
> Octavio: What is dawn?
> Helena: It's a bee buzzing inside your eyes. What is living together?
> Octavio: It's laughing without knowing quite why.
> Helena: What is intelligence?
> Octavio: It's entering the abyss with your eyes open. What is madness?
> Helena: It's inventing a hieroglyph.

Octavio: What is baptismal water?

Helena: It's a dove mounted on a tiger.

Lucinda: What is a psychiatrist?

Helena: It's a kite guided by a blind person.

Portilla: What is the love of a ballerina?

Helena: It's falling into a trap that doesn't trap.

Portilla: What is true love?

Helena: It's coming home at midnight and finding midday.

A. Burns: What is Helena's thought?

Helena: It's traveling on a flying carpet.

C. Fuentes: What is the labyrinth of solitude?

Helena: It's the closure of the entrance to Hell.

C. Fuentes: What is puberty?

Helena: It's sitting waiting for the meteor shower.

A. Burns: What is a schoolgirl?

La Chatita: It's a *fil de la Vierge*.

THREE YELLOW TULIPS

Silvina Ocampo and Bioy Casares had no biological offspring (Marta Bioy Ocampo [1954–1994], whom Silvina adopted, was Casares's biological daughter with a lover he called María Teresa) and Bioy was very keen to have a child with Elena. In his letters, he says he wants to write to his mother to tell her that he's found a "poetic and magical" person who has "offered [him] a son." He reiterates how much he'd love "that boy we talked about in the Luxembourg Garden."

Elena Garro Papers.

But Elena's pregnancy complicated matters—even more. On the one hand, it seems that Bioy offered to set up a home for Elena and her daughter in Montevideo. And in several statements, Elena says that Paz initially decided to give her the freedom to be with Bioy but then changed his mind. "That child is legally mine. When it's born, I'll send it to my mother. And if you go off with Bioy, you'll never see Elena again because I'm the diplomat and the one with the power. The embassy will support me. You poor stupid woman!" According to Helena Paz, those were her father's words.

Testimonios sobre Elena Garro, p. 216.

Memorias, p. 199.

In *Testimonios sobre Mariana*, there's a scene that is very similar to Helena Paz's account:

Testimonios sobre Mariana, p. 176.

> "Mariana, we're married, and if you'd had that child, legally it would be mine. If you'd filed for divorce, the child would still have been mine, legally speaking, for a year after the decree absolute."
> "And what if I were to tell the truth?" she asked.
> "It would make no difference. The child would be legally mine."
> "So, the truth doesn't matter in the law?"
> "Mariana, the law is the truth."
> "I don't understand..."
> "That's one of your charms," he said.

There's also a scene in which Mariana and her lover, Vicente, are making the decision to abort:

Ibid., p. 61.

> Nobody passed close by us, we were completely alone deciding on the life or death of a third person and speculating about its appearance... The deep secret of life and death was with us; they were the two oldest and the originating miracles of the world, but we modern humans rarely think of them.

In the end, Elena had an abortion with her general practitioner, Dr. Lievain, without the presence of either of the men. The abortion, which wasn't Elena's first, was done illegally, as all abortions were at that time. Heaven knows what circumstances it was performed in, and the outcome was almost fatal for Elena, both physically and emotionally.

In Helena Paz's testimony, it would seem that the decision to abort was solely due to her father's attitude, but Laura Ramos recalls Elena telling her that Paz was afraid Bioy would seduce his daughter, Helena: "She was already grown up [Helena was around twelve], and Octavio said that Bioy wanted us both as lovers. He was crazy! Said I'd soon see how Bioy looked at Helena, undressing her with his eyes!" By contrast, Bioy's letters display a level of guilt, which suggests that he did in fact want Elena to abort.

Elena Garro: Los recuerdos sin porvenir (Elena Garro: Recollections Without a Future), p. 92.

In their correspondence, Bioy often refers to that unborn child as "El Charro," the cowboy. (For them, this ideal baby is male, in the same way as Elena and Paz had imagined Felipe.) El Charro is part of a personal mythology Bioy and Elena constructed, an amorous lexicon that includes, among other things, the shoe Bioy lost one day in the countryside and other suitors they called their "shadows." In one letter, Bioy says, "I know that nothing can cleanse me of the twofold sin of not allowing El Charro to come into the world and of abandoning you that awful August of loneliness and fever."

Elena Garro Papers.

In Elena's books, this episode of her life is symbolized by three yellow tulips. Three flowers that are her, Bioy, and the lost son; the illusion of a family that never was. One poem says:

Cristales de tiempo, p. 168.

Three yellow tulips
launch pale flames in the evening.
Six tulips
with the three in the mirror,
flaming coldly, closed,
keep watch over the absence
your face leaves
this evening.

And in *Testimonios sobre Mariana*:

Testimonios sobre Mariana, p. 74.

I found her in bed, looking at a vase over the hearth with three yellow tulips that were reflected in the mirror.

"There are three of us," she said.

In an interview, Lucía Melgar asks Elena why Bioy left her.

Lectura múltiple, p. 299.

EG: Because he didn't want to leave Silvina.
LM: But was it that he loved her so deeply or was there some other reason?
EG: He once said something very strange to me: "Do you understand what it means to be married to an Ocampo?" And I said, "No, I don't."

Memorias, p. 199.

The Ocampo family belonged to the Argentinian aristocracy and were a power base in the cultural milieu of the country. According to Helena Paz's memoir, Bioy was furious after the abortion and left for the south of France with Silvina. On his return, he saw Elena one more time, on August 9, 1951, and two days later he traveled back to Buenos Aires. Bioy's later letters continue to insist on a possible future together. He asks Elena to marry him, invites her to La Plata or Buenos Aires, but nothing ever comes of these fantasies. Helena Paz says that at one point her mother found out that Bioy, who swore her fidelity and "celibacy," had gotten another woman pregnant. That finally shattered her illusions.

On June 5, 1952, Paz was transferred to Japan. He moved into a hotel and sent Elena an ultimatum: "If the two of you aren't here in Japan within the month, there will be consequences." Despite being afraid of traveling, Elena obeyed his diktat. She had the vast number of required vaccinations, set sail, and arrived in Tokyo suffering from myelitis. The abortion, on top of so many vaccinations, had resulted in an infection. In her *Memorias*, Helena recounts that her mother felt so ill one day that she asked for Dr. Fukase to be called (they knew him from the time Paz fell from a hotel balcony; he survived but was badly injured). "I'm dying," said Elena. Octavio was unwilling to call the doctor: "There's nothing wrong with you. It's just your usual histrionics." Helena then ran to the telephone and called the front desk to ask for help. Paz was so furious, he hit her on the forehead with the telephone, hard enough for the wound to bleed. Dr. Fukase arrived and checked on the two Elenas. When he examined the older of the two, he said, in broken English, "The lady is passin' away." He nevertheless succeeded in stabilizing her condition but warned that

Ibid., pp. 253-4.

she needed immediate treatment that wasn't available in Japan. After a difficult battle with the Mexican embassy and a telegram that Elena sent to President Miguel Alemán (saying that if they weren't transferred, she would die in Japan, in which case would they please cut her into small pieces to make it easier to send her body back to Mexico), they succeeded in being transferred to Berne. During her convalescence, Paz recommended that she write about her childhood, and there, with a Remington on her lap, Elena composed her first novel—unpublished until ten years later: *Recollections of Things to Come*.

Ibid., p. 282.

RECOLLECTIONS OF THINGS TO COME

Elena Garro's most famous novel makes literature of her childhood in Iguala. It deals with the struggle of a small town to maintain its traditions and religion during the Cristera War and is a treatise on time: the congealed time of tragedy, the cyclical time of wars, the impossible time of ghosts. It's the story of two women, Isabel and Julia, who suffered under the violence of an authoritarian regime and deep-rooted machismo, in the form of General Francisco Rosas. It's the story of a femicide, of the ghost of one woman and another who has been turned to stone. It's the vindication of the miraculous possibilities of theater. It's the story of a betrayal. It's the invention of a geographical space and its people. *Recollections of Things to Come* is the memory, voice, story, and history of the town of Ixtepec.

IMPRESSIONS OF JAPAN

In a letter to Pepe Bianco, Elena writes:

José Bianco Papers.

> I can tell you almost nothing about the Japanese: the men are sometimes good-looking and always short. The language is difficult because it doesn't resemble anything else. The women are either horrible or quite lovely. The landscape is gorgeous, a sort of Austria with little paper houses. The food is raw, except for tempura, which was brought by the Spanish, and fried fish.

And shortly afterward, in the same letter, she says:

> Japan is the end of the world, but I'm even further off, I'm in the country of fear. When I'm awake I'm spying on myself, when I'm asleep I dream that I'm still spying on myself.

DEATH OF THE HEROES

There was a time when Elena idealized love. In her play *La señora en su balcón* (The Lady on her Balcony), the protagonist outlines the utopia of a perfect, eternal love:

> No, what I want is an agreement to continue living inseparably together forever after life has ended. Like what has been seen and memory, like man and his unchangeable past, like the positive and negative that together make lightning. I'm asking you for the will to be one.

Teatro completo, p. 88.

In 1936, in a letter to Paz, she expresses the sense of having lost that ideal:

> I cried for the Elena of a year ago, for all the young people who fail every day; for all women who aspire to experiencing love in the way I understood and desired it: enormous, joyful, absolute, in harmony with the infinite.

Cristales de tiempo, p. 39.

And from then on, when she talks or writes about love, disenchantment prevails. In an interview with Patricia Rosas Lopátegui, she says, "Love never worked out for me, I think that love is very difficult in the world we live in..." To José Antonio Cordero, she says that she was never "very deeply in love," that, for her, love is like a pipe dream "because living together always turns out to be a failure. And when love is true, like in novels or history, the heroes die." When Lucía Melgar asks what love means for her, she responds, "Well, it was seeing something so marvelous, so extensive, where everything seems lovely: a tree is a divine tree, a house...everything is lovely. But when you find yourself alone, it seems it was all very ordinary."

Ibid., p. 54.

La cuarta casa.

Lectura múltiple, p. 299.

ANOTHER QUESTION GAME

Elena devised a universe with parallel times, in which the present, past, and future coexisted and it was possible to recollect things yet to come. In that universe, it must also be possible to divine the past. As I'm still filled with doubts in relation to Elena, I decide to perform my own divinations about her past.

First, I asked a few friends to play the question game with me:

Jazmina: Who is Elena Garro?
Isabel: It's something that deserves to be translated.

Jazmina: What was going on in her head?
Jorge: It's a ripped painting.

Jazmina: Who's to blame for what happened to her?
Aurelia: It's a wasp without a stinger.

Jazmina: What about her daughter?
Marina: It's the torture of undeserved pain.

Jazmina: What can we know about her?
César: It's a dog that's unhappy because its owner isn't there.

Jazmina: What can't we know about her?
Elisa: The past seen backlit.

EVERYTHING ELSE IS BRUTISH

The first time Elena considered taking her own life appears to have been when she married Paz and had the urge to throw herself on the tramlines. Her diary entries mention two other attempts in Paris, with gas and a cord. In *Testimonios sobre Mariana*, the description of the protagonist's two suicide attempts is almost identical to those accounts. Mariana, however, achieves her aim on the third attempt by jumping from a fifth-floor window, taking her daughter with her. Her ghost still roams this world, seeking to redeem her sin. As Elena was a Catholic, that must have been what suicide was: a sin.

In the diaries, there is more than one reference to the temptation to commit suicide. In 1945, for example: "I dread returning to Octavio. Not that he's asked me to: he's always saying that I'm going to commit suicide, maybe the time has come." In 1948, she writes, "Suicide seems the only logical solution. Everything else is brutish and so stupid." And in 1960, when Helena lived for a short time with her father: "I don't have a cent to my name. Suicide is difficult. I've thought

Testimonios sobre Elena Garro, p. 157.

José Bianco Papers.

about it and it's complicated. Maybe pills. Octavio is like a mad dog: he kicked Chata. Then he called me to announce, 'Your daughter is unbearable.' I arranged to see her in Le Relais Plaza. She cried a lot."

Testimonios sobre Elena Garro, p. 241.

Elena also recalls in her diaries that, after their divorce, Octavio Paz encouraged her to commit suicide. "I remember that when I put him up in my apartment in Paris, he begged me to commit suicide so he could have something good to say about me: 'Kill yourself, Helencitos, then I can write and say that you were a marvelous woman, that you were poetry incarnate, a genius.'" Elena asks herself why, as a newlywed, she used to find Gillette blades under her pillow.

Ibid., p. 423.

Ibid., p. 419.

DREAM CURE

In Geneva in 1953, Elena's treatment regime was changed and she was prescribed a "dream cure" for a month. Every morning, she had breakfast, took a pill, and slept until night. When she woke, she had dinner, took another pill, and slept until morning. According to Helena, after that month of sleeping, she was cured. In the meanwhile, Paz was falling in love with the Italian painter and author Bona Tibertelli.

Memorias, p. 286.

That same year, Paz was offered a post in the Foreign Ministry and the family returned to Mexico. During the journey, Elena had a shipboard romance with the captain of the boat. He tried to convince her to run away with him, but she wasn't interested. The affair served as the inspiration for the short story "La vida empieza a las tres" ("Life Begins at Three"). When they arrived in Mexico, Elena and Paz rented an apartment on Avenida Insurgentes, at the intersection with Viaducto Miguel Alemán, and then moved to Calle Nuevo León 230 in the Condesa neighborhood. Their home soon became a salon for the cultural community.

Ibid., p. 306.

The crème de la crème: Luis Bruñuel, Salvador Elizondo, Carlos Fuentes, Luis Villoro, and Elena Poniatowska were among the many guests. By all accounts, Elena Garro was an amusing hostess and, seduced by her beauty, all eyes would be on her as she told her stories and jokes and impersonated others to a rapt audience.

At the same time, Elena was writing more and more. She did a lot of research into the revolutionary leader Felipe Ángeles, a character who had until then been sidelined in the official history. Using the material she gathered, she wrote a play that describes how easily the revolution was corrupted once its aims had been achieved. She also wrote articles and a series of biographical polemics about leading characters in the Mexican Revolution. While all this was going on, her marriage—by then a (more or less) strategic alliance—continued to limp from crisis to crisis, separations and reunions. She'd spend days, whole weeks without talking to Paz. In addition, during that period, Elena began a relationship with the filmmaker Archibaldo Burns, while Paz's relationships with Bona Tibertelli and other women continued.

There was a particularly difficult time after the death of her cousin and childhood accomplice, Boni, on December 28, 1953. The official theory is that he committed suicide, but Elena was certain he'd been murdered. In her diaries, she repeatedly says that she's thinking of Boni, dreaming of him.

TURTLES

The Princeton archives close at four in the afternoon and after that I meet up with the ambassadors on the benches outside the library before we go to find something to eat—from nine to four we don't take our noses out of the old papers and we leave with our stomachs rumbling loudly. During the meal, we exchange gossip. The authors we're researching were more-or-less contemporaries; I found a mention of Donoso in Elena's letters; Donoso's ambassador found several meetings with Pitol in the diaries; and Pitol's ambassador came across a couple of mentions of Octavio Paz that say, "Paz is undoubtedly one of the best Spanish prose writers" and "he has become one the most deeply hated figures in Mexico. Pride and arrogance have been his downfall." Virgilio Piñera's ambassador is going to allow us to have a peek at the archive of Pepe Bianco, who seemed to have a finger in every pie and corresponded with the whole world. I'm trying to persuade Pizarnik's ambassador to let me have a look at her archive because I've been told that each of the diaries is a work of art. In them, Pizarnik writes about her beloved Silvina Ocampo, the truly brilliant, eccentric writer who never seemed to have displayed the least jealousy of Elena Garro or any of the many other lovers of her husband, Bioy Casares.

After that meal, we walk down to see the river for the first time. As we approach, we see signs warning motorists of turtles crossing. We continue on to the riverbank and stop at a small delta, where the waters split into separate channels. In the early evening light, we see several huge turtles swimming there.

LAND AND LIBERTY

In 1958, in the offices of the Fondo de Cultura Económica in Mexico City, an elegant farewell party was arranged for the writer Rómulo Gallegos, who was returning to his home in Venezuela. Elena Garro arrived at the event accompanied by a group of campesinos from the town of Ahuatepec, Morelos State. They were hoping to gather signatures from the illustrious guests to demand a halt to the seizure of their land and the outbreak of violence and repression against the peasants. Arnaldo Orfila, the director of the organization and guest of honor, and the other intellectuals all refused to sign. Elena and the campesinos sat for a bit to listen to the hypocritical, leftist speeches given from the podium but left before the end of the event. Once outside, they found chauffeurs keeping watch over the expensive cars and, with their complicity, Elena and the campesinos went from car to car puncturing the tires.

Elena Garro, la pérdida del reino, p. 38.

Poniatowska, *Obras reunidas* (Collected Works), p. 90.

Elena had always been a supporter of agrarian reform (perhaps not as a very young child, but I wouldn't bet on it) and the issue of the distribution of land runs through many of her works, from *Recollections of Things to Come* to *Felipe Ángeles.* She said that one evening in 1958, two campesinos, Antonia Ramiréz and Enedino Montiel, appeared at her door (possibly sent by a lawyer who had already told Elena their story) to ask for her help: they wanted her to plead their case before the former president Lázaro Cárdenas in the matter of a millionaire who was trying to appropriate their land. Elena says that when she saw their "cracked feet" in her living room, she felt like a "terrible sinner." So she decided to help them and took their cause seriously; she supported their struggle with rigorous newspaper articles, with her presence at the Departamento de Asuntos Agrarios y Colonización and in the offices of the Confederación Nacional Campesina (CNC), plus appearances in court and at demonstrations.

Lectura múltiple, p. 327.

Together with her sister Deva and her husband, the painter Jesús Guerrero Galván—both communists—she backed strikes and supported the Morelos leader Rubén Jaramillo until he, his pregnant wife, and their children were assassinated in Xochicalco. Deva and her family constructed a tomb for the family and the Princeton archive includes the invitation to the funeral. Rumor has it that Elena slapped the governor of Morelos State's face after the murders.

Ibid., pp. 146 and 274-5.

In interviews, Elena claimed that an attempt was made to poison her daughter during that time, and Archibaldo Burns was shot at for "hanging around with the blonde." Both survived the attempts on their lives.

She also became friendly with some young

members of the Communist Party, who occasionally asked her to hide other friends, as she did not long before 1968 for Raúl Palacios, the young man they nicknamed "Piñata" after he arrived home badly wounded. Elena fictionalized the story of "Piñata" in her brilliant but disturbing novel *Y Matarazo no llamó* (And Matarazo Didn't Call).

Garro, *Obras reunidas III* (Collected Works III), p. xxiv.

After the tribunal in which Enedino Montiel, with her assistance, managed to recover various properties in Ahuatepec, Elena said—and this seems likely—President Lopéz Mateos himself recommended that Paz should send his wife out of the country. Paz, who had once supported Elena's involvement in the agrarian struggle, had by then had enough of his spouse's political stridency, which did nothing to help his diplomatic career. In addition, he was deeply in love with Bona Tibertelli and they had both promised to get divorced so they could be together.

DOING HER JUSTICE

This journey to the *Elena Garro Papers* has cost me an arm and a leg: I was too late to apply for the grant the university offers to help finance research in its archives; I couldn't find anybody to put me up in Princeton; the flight and the hotel room have cost double the advance I received for the book. And there are times when none of this makes any sense. Just what else can I learn about Elena Garro? Just what else can I say? Haven't I gotten the main points clear now? Haven't all the books I've read been enough? No, they haven't. They gave me a jigsaw puzzle with pieces missing, the ruins of a temple that has been looted thousands of times, and I'm determined to believe that every single item I recover, however small, is important. Important to me. Instead of resigning myself to not understanding, to accepting that there's no such thing as fully understanding a living person, let alone a dead one, and even less so such a chaotic dead woman as this one, I go on trying to find another clue, a piece, however tiny, that turns out to be the key to doing her justice. Because, to be frank, that's all I'm interested in: doing her justice.

FORGET IT

That stuff about doing her justice is so pretentious! Elena doesn't need me. Better just to admit it once and for all: I'm writing this book for myself.

THE CRIME OF FANTASY

Sometimes, when people said her work was a precursor of magical realism, she'd get irritated and say there was no such thing, that, in any case, it was fantastic literature; or that there was nothing magical about what she'd written, reality was like that; or that she was sick of magical realism, of so much magic, so many tricks. But other times she agreed: she said she had been a precursor, that magic was a device she used in her books when she couldn't find any other way to get out of a jam. She'd say that García Márquez had read her work and had perhaps even borrowed certain elements of *Recollections* for his *One Hundred Years of Solitude* (the yellow butterflies, for instance), and this despite the Columbian telling her he thought *Recollections* was as kitsch as an embroidered handkerchief.

Lectura múltiple, p. 292.

Elena had her own particular way of understanding the supernatural. She said she believed in ghosts and miracles. She adored Novalis: "He was the one who formulated the idea that we are more closely connected to the invisible than to the visible." In her work, no doubt is ever cast on the supernatural,

Cristales de tiempo, p. 52.

it causes no surprise; like the miraculous elements of fairy tales, the myths and legends of indigenous peoples, it is accepted as part of reality.

In *Testimonios sobre Mariana*, Gabrielle says, "His words convinced me that toying with the miraculous is not only dangerous but invites ridicule. Everyday reality measures actions and facts with the narrow yardstick of so-called common sense, and common sense cheapens fantasy to the point of making it a crime."

Testimonios sobre Mariana, p. 193.

HATEFUL

I find Bioy Casares's handwriting illegible, but I can understand Elena's because it's identical to my grandmother's. My great-grandfather and Elena's grandmother lived on the same street in Mexico City as I live on now. Elena was born a few years before my grandmother, but there's something in the tone of her voice, the phrases, sayings, and proverbs she uses, in the way she poses for photographs, that reminds me so much of my grandmother. A little while ago, when I visited my great-aunt Lolín, who is over ninety-one and loves reading, I asked if she'd ever read Elena Garro. She can hardly speak these days, but she nodded. When I asked what she thought of her, she made a huge effort to whisper decisively, "hateful."

ARCHIBALDO BURNS

Her relationship with Archibaldo Burns was—just for a change—complex. On the positive side, Burns supported her in her activities with the campesinos and they worked together on movie projects. He took inspiration from one of the short stories in *Semana de colores* for his documentary film *Perfecto Luna* (sadly, never distributed). And when Elena had to leave Mexico in 1959, she first lived with Burns and later, in 1961, in an apartment that may have been bought by Helena using Burns's money (she said that it was money she stole from Burns and used to buy the apartment in exchange for not revealing some horrific secrets).

Debo olvidar que existí (I Must Forget That I Existed), p. 112.

Nevertheless, Elena wrote to Pepe Bianco that "on two furious occasions, he crashed two cars with the two of us inside. I never loved him. Why? Who knows! I'm sure he's planning my death at this very instant." She said that he stalked her, although he obviously helped her at times. Elena also mentions in her diary the day she found out that Burns had had sexual relations with Gérard Genevois in her bed, while she was away on a trip. There are traces of these stories—transformed,

José Bianco Papers.

Testimonios sobre Elena Garro, p. 243.

invented, and mixed with characters from the books of F. Scott Fitzgerald and Evelyn Waugh—in her eerie thriller *Reencuento de personajes* (Reunion of Characters). She later told Bianco that she'd set her grudges against Archibaldo aside and had started to remember him as just a good friend and accomplice: "It would be too sad if God were to take us up at this instant and call us to account. 'And what did you do with the talents I gave you?' Me: fight with Octavio Paz and run away from Archi Burns."

José Bianco Papers.

THE TRUNKS

Elena Garro's six legendary trunks containing her letters, diaries, photos, and manuscripts traveled around the world with her. They were left in hotels and recovered later. The (many) manuscripts in them survived untimely departures, imposter syndrome, her violent relationship with Paz, and incendiary threats. Some of the contents of those trunks ended up in the fourteen boxes stored in the Princeton archive: in the yellow cardboard box in front of me. It's said that the trunks reached a combined weight of 360 pounds, but I've found no evidence anywhere of who carried them or how they were transported on all those journeys when she had no money.

Elena Garro, la pérdida del reino, p. 65.

PASSIONATE INDIFFERENCE

In February 1957, Elena saw Bioy Casares for the last time. Both Bioy and Paz had been invited to New York for an event at the United Nations and Elena went there to join Paz and her daughter, who had preceded her.

Memorias, pp. 419-30.

Helena Paz describes the difficulties Elena and Bioy had in meeting in New York due to Paz's absolute ban on any encounter. On one occasion, Helena had to invite Bioy secretly to a party for them to see one another. Paz also contacted Archibaldo Burns in Mexico and ordered him to come to New York and put a stop to their meeting. Elena lied, slipped away quietly, and once even jumped across the tables of a restaurant (or so says Helena, but I find it hard to imagine the acrobatic prowess needed) to escape and go see him.

Ibid., p. 442.

Helena also says that toward the end of the New York trip, she took Bioy to a café where she knew Elena and Paz were so they could say their farewells. There's a photograph of that scene, the only one I know where Elena and Bioy appear together. The two of them are sitting on one side of the table, with Octavio and Helena Paz on the other. Helena writes that her father was angry and kept glaring at her, but in the photo they are all smiling. In her diary entry of February 6 of that year, Elena notes that she dined with Bioy and Octavio:

> Old Bioy is a paradigm: with his thinning blond hair, his gold chain, his beautiful, borrowed manners, his pouting lower lip, and his rounded shoulders, he's the perfect representative of nothingness. What does freedom mean when it's spoken? Nothing. What does hunger mean? Nothing. Maybe he and all the financial benefits he's accrued from learning that lexicon… Who gave him so many privileges? A million cows, another million billy goats, the goatherds, the cowboys he has in the Pampas.

Testimonios sobre Elena Garro, p. 226.

She still admits to Bioy's attractions: "He's intelligent, handsome, is always very well-dressed; his facial expressions are carefully discreet, he's in control of his gaze, his smile, he conscientiously cultivates his limitations with unbridled coquetry." However, there is now irony, an inviolable critical distance in that admission: "One would say he was the perfect lover if I hadn't been told by him and everyone who knows him about his innumerable adventures with the typists and married women he nourishes with chocolates and disdain in the garçonnières of Buenos Aires."

Ibid., p. 228.

In another diary entry Elena transcribes a conversation she had with Bioy during that trip, which is so comical that she later paraphrases it in *Testimonios sobre Mariana*:

Testimonios sobre Elena Garro, p. 229.

> "Helena, my beloved."
>
> "The thing is, Bioy, you gave me such a good lesson that I can't be in love with anyone now."
>
> "Me neither, Helena. Not with anyone because there's no one like you. Ay, that's so true; there's no one, no other Helena in the whole world. Look…seeing you was like having a fever, living in a world of madness, of fever. I can't, I can't be in love with anyone else either."
>
> "I believe you, Bioy, but what I'm saying is with anyone at all, not even Bioy."

Despite that snub, she's concerned about the final impression she will leave on Bioy. She bought a black skirt, an Italian black velveteen blouse, a white chiffon scarf, and pearls. She wanted to "look pretty to say farewell." And she writes in her diary, "I'd repeated to myself so often that I'd be indifferent, that it wasn't hard. Pleasant, passionate indifference."

Ibid., p. 230.

Decades later, in an interview, she would say about her last meeting with Bioy: "I saw him in New York…but, there you are…it had all died."

Lectura múltiple, p. 299.

DIVORCE IN JUÁREZ

In March 1957, after a biopsy, Elena was told that she needed to have her fallopian tubes, ovaries, uterus, and cervix removed. In her diary, she writes that it was a shock, she was scared.

Testimonios sobre Elena Garro, p. 230.

That same year, Paz helped to arrange premiers of three of her works: *Andarse por las ramas* (Beating Around the Bush), *Los pilares de doña Blanca* (Doña Blanca's Pillars), and *Un hogar sólido*. They were staged in the fourth Poesía en Voz Alta (Spoken Word Poetry) program to critical acclaim. Those three short, stunning pieces, which blended popular children's songs, nonsense humor, surrealism, and ghost stories, set the tone for her first book, *Un hogar sólido*, a compilation of seven one-act plays, published in 1958 by the Universidad Veracruzana.

That debut publication appeared when she was forty-one, an age that might now seem late, but in those times it wasn't unusual for female writers who were also mothers—bearing the brunt of domestic chores and childcare—to delay publishing until their offspring (and husbands) needed less attention.

Obra poética (Poetic Works), p. 259.

1957 was also the year Paz moved out of their home for good (to live with his mother) and started writing *Piedra de sol* (*Sunstone*), his most famous poem, in which he lavishes praise on his lover Bona Tibertelli and describes Elena as a Circe, a Melusine, "a pelt that hangs from a pack of bones." Elena would later write to him in a letter, "You said I was Circe. You're the best proof of it, you pig."

Elena Garro Papers.

The divorce was finally processed by Paz in 1959, in Cuidad Juárez, without Elena's knowledge, taking advantage of a law in Chihuahua State that allowed unilateral divorce. Such proceedings were later ruled to be invalid, thus further complicating the legal status of a marriage that was possibly never valid in the first place since Elena was underage.

Rather than an ending, this was merely the start of a new phase in the interminable battles of that quarrelsome pair. Elena complained that when they separated, she was left with a pathetic share of their property, "a 160-peso couch, two Salinas y Rocha beds, six chairs from his bachelor pad with torn upholstery...I didn't have the right to any of the bookcases or even a book." She said that the judge was unaware that the marriage had been registered under the "joint property" ruling and deprived her of all her belongings. According to Elena, the divorce litigation was never resolved.

Testimonios sobre Elena Garro, p. 235.

But in spite of everything, the former couple enjoyed a brief period of friendship in France. Paz was living in Paris, and the Elenas moved in to an apartment there at the end of the year. Elena even put him

Octavio Paz en su siglo (Octavio Paz in His Century), p. 377.

up in her home for several months after Bona Tibertelli "swapped Mexicans" by leaving him for the painter Francisco Toledo.

ON THE LONELINESS OF THE DEVIL

She was never absolutely alone for long. First, she lived with her family and then with Octavio Paz, and then, until the end of her life, with her daughter. But as we all know, it's possible to experience great loneliness, even when surrounded by others. Then there was the blow of passing from a life led in public to ostracism, from large dinner dances to unhealthy confinement.

Lectura múltiple, p. 199.

Even so, in an interview she said, "The thing is, I've never felt lonely. I'm very much alone because I like being alone. Because when I'm alone, here for example, I start thinking, imagining, loving things, friends, my cats... Solitude, being alone, doesn't feel tragic to me. It's tragic for the devil because he lacks affection."

NOBODY IN THE WORLD

Elena lived with her daughter and seven cats on Rue de l'Ancienne-Commédie from 1959 to 1963. It was an elegant apartment that had once been the lobby of the Comédie-Française. She was interviewed there by Elena Poniatowska, who described the opulence and impressive glamour of the place with a wealth of detail.

El asesinato de Elena Garro, p. 126.

After that, she moved to an apartment that had not been completely refurbished, where she had an experience that she tells Pepe Bianco about in a letter, and which formed the basis of her novel *Mi hermanita Magdalena* (My Little Sister Magdalena): a member of the OAS (Organisation armée secrète, a French, far-right terrorist group) left a trunk filled with documents and compromising letters in her apartment, and she was afraid both of keeping it and of being branded an informer if she handed it in to the police. She said that when she decided on the latter course of action, the people linked to the documents began to be arrested.

José Bianco Papers.

Apart from their brief moment of friendship in Paris, the roller coaster of her relationship with Paz was in a nosedive. In another letter to Bianco, she says:

Ibid.

> During the two months Chatita lived with him in the embassy, he did such awful things (for example, not opening the front door when she came back from parties and so leaving her in the street the whole night, hitting her, slandering her, etc.) that she got really ill. She was covered in eczema and on the verge of a nervous collapse.

Testimonios sobre Elena Garro, p. 241.

In 1962, she received that call from Archibaldo Burns, informing her of the murder of her friends Enedino Montiel and Antonia Ramírez. In a letter to Pepe Bianco, Elena described her feelings:

José Bianco Papers.

> The government murdered them for their land. The news made me ill. Since then, events continue to be disturbing but I don't know what to do to defend them. What are you supposed to do when they kill women and children?[...] They gouge out their eyes, stuff dirt in their mouths, and so on. Awful, just awful.

CREDO

Elena's Catholicism came mostly from her father's side of the family; he'd come close to being ordained as a priest. "God is my fellow man, trees, animals, you, me. God is what controls life and death. God is order and justice," says the protagonist of *Felipe Ángeles*. In the archive, there's a church pamphlet with the times of services, and her diaries show she attended mass regularly and frequently prayed. On a couple of occasions, when she was forced into hiding, she took refuge in convents. She wrote a novel with a nun as the main character: *Inés*. She used to say that she was not so much a Catholic as a Guadalupana and devotee of St. Michael the Archangel. But she wasn't married in a church, had lovers, abortions, got divorced, and attempted suicide. This may be why Archibaldo Burns said that Elena's Catholicism could be taken on and off like a wig.

Teatro completo, p. 241.

Lectura múltiple, p. 137.

Her father introduced her to Buddhism. When they passed through Ceylon (now Sri Lanka) on their way to Japan, Helena was surprised by how familiar her mother was with Buddhist codes and customs.

Memorias, p. 231.

In his documentary *La cuarta casa*, José Antonio Cordero asks Elena what she believes in. And she responds with this credo:

> I believe in Dostoyevsky.
> I believe in Turgenev.
> I believe in Teresa of Ávila.
> I believe in Ernst Jünger.
> In everything.
> In God and in the Devil.
> In the angels and demons.
> In saints, I believe firmly.
> Well, I believe in the Greek gods too.

PERFUME

I believe in the ghost of Elena Garro, in my imaginary memory where she laughs at her own jokes, where she is young, dresses in beige, and smells of cigarettes, cats, and French perfume.

RAGE

After their divorce, Paz became a great promotor of Elena's work. In 1963, he convinced Joaquín Mortiz to publish *Los recuerdos del porvenir* (*Recollections of Things to Come*), and with Paz as a member of the jury, the novel was awarded the prestigious Premio Xavier Villaurrutia.

Toward the end of 1963, Elena Garro returned from Paris to Mexico and Paz went to New Delhi as ambassador to India. While they remained in contact, I can find no record that they met in person for the rest of their lives.

Testimonios sobre Elena Garro, p. 253.

In that same year, Elena had a raging argument with her cousin, the ballerina Amalia Hernández, over the movie *Solo de noche vienes* (You Only Come at Night). (I refuse to write the extra paragraphs needed to explain a dispute that seems to me more tiresome than relevant.) She was also bitten by a rabid dog outside a pharmacy and had to be vaccinated.

In 1964, the Universidad Veracruzana published her collection of short stories, *La semana de colores*.

A CHROMATIC SCALE

Blue

The diary she wrote as an adolescent makes several references to wearing blue. The dress she was wearing when she met Paz was blue, and that is why he calls her "girl in blue" and "the color blue, my very breath" in his letters. The notebooks containing her Spanish diaries are blue, as are the letters sent to her by Bioy: blue envelopes, and inside, blue ink on sky-blue paper (he also used to wear a blue mariner's cap). And the letters from her friend José Bianco were also blue; "hope is blue," she wrote to him. And:

Memorias, p. 190.

> Do you remember how handsome Bioy was? Strange that he has lumbago. I don't know what it is. In any case, I see that illness as a slightly steely blue, like plumbago, a flower I used to love as a child, when it covered the garden walls. Typical of Bioy to get a flower sickness.

José Bianco Papers.

Cuentos Completos (Complete Short Stories), pp. 449 and 470.

"What was it like to be happy?" Lucy, the protagonist of the short story "Hoy es jueves" (Today is Thursday) asks herself as she "vaguely recalled blue days, fluvial days." Blue—her father had told her—suited her because it's "for the blondes."

The final episode of *Andamos huyendo, Lola* tells the story of a woman named (or renamed) Dionisia, who is desperately seeking a cut turquoise where she used to live. That is where the following words appear: "Listen! A stateless woman can't go around the way you do, all dressed in blue."

Andamos huyendo, Lola, p. 350.

Green

Testimonios sobre Elena Garro, p. 334.

When Helena Paz had to undergo surgery in 1973, Elena Garro hid a green heart in her hair, like an amulet.

Beige

El asesinato de Elena Garro, p. 126.

She is often described wearing shades of beige, gold, and caramel (in the early days of their love affair, Paz fills his poems with references to gold). In her diaries, she says that she tended to go for white or beige. Poniatowska describes her apartment in France as having "all the tones of burnt sugar," with "coffee-colored armchairs, beige rugs, tobacco-colored chairs." She says that "surrounded by the pure colors that suit her best, Elena is a ray of light; her hair forms a halo of sun and autumn."

Rainbow

In *Andamos huyendo, Lola,* one of the characters classifies her memories by color:

> Yes, her lost memory was blue, dotted with flurries of snow, blizzards, shards of glass, and spirals of hail. Perhaps there are different colored memories. Memories as green as honeysuckle, and memories as red as cardinals' vestments. And there were also memories as yellow as sunflowers or the robes of Buddhist monks. She'd seen them, and their elongated figures had a frozen mandarin in the center under a torrent of hyacinths...

Andamos huyendo, Lola, p. 338.

In the disturbing title story of *La semana de colores*, each day of the week is both a woman and a color. The two young girls in the story witness a femicide and the week becomes disordered for them, as do the colors.

THE WEEK OF COLORS

Almost every day, *La semana de colores* is my favorite of Elena Garro's books. It contains her most famous short story, "La culpa es de los tlaxcaltecas" (The Tlatcaltecas Are to Blame), which can be read as a restructuring of the story of Malinche, the woman who translated for Cortés during the Conquest and who has been the object of innumerable histories, myths, and legends in Mexico. In this story, the protagonist is a woman who lives a double life in two parallel time zones—the twentieth century and the era of the Conquest—and the narrative addresses the idea of betrayal, of what women's betrayal means in a world of men.

In that book there is also a group of stories based on Elena's childhood memories in Iguala: "El día que fuimos perros" (The Day We Were Dogs), "La semana de colores," "Antes de la Guerra de Troya" (Before the Trojan War), "El robo de Titzla" (The Titzla Robbery), "El duende" (The Elf), and "Nuestras vidas son ríos" (Our Lives are Rivers). In all these stories, the magical perception of young girls blends with the vision of the indigenous peoples of Iguala and that mix gives rise to a series of fantastic adventures, as enchanting as they are unsettlingly dark.

The book also includes some of the best stories expressing social criticism and condemnation in Elena's oeuvre: "El árbol" (The Tree), "El zapaterito de Guanajuato" (The Little Shoemaker of Guanajuato), and "Perfecto Luna"(Perfecto Luna). It has been compared to the work of Juan Rulfo, but Margo Glantz says that *La semana de colores* has a crucial difference from Rulfo: what we would now call "gender perspective."

'Elena Garro: El color de la muerte" (Elena Garro: The Color of Death).

CINEMA AND FOOLISHNESS

It was her good friend Julio Bracho who taught her how to write screenplays. [*Lectura múltiple*, p. 289.] The first one she did was *Historia de un gran amor* (The Story of a Great Love), an adaptation of Antonio de Alarcón's novel *El niño de la bola* (The Child of the Ball). She liked the finished product, saying, "That movie was nice in its moment." [*Hispamérica*, p. 58.] She also wrote the screenplays for *Las ratas* (The Rats) by José Bianco and *En memoria de Paulina* (In Memory of Paulina) by Bioy Casares, plus other such adaptations as *La escondida* (The Woman in Hiding) and *Renuncia a la gloria* (Renouncing Glory); however, none of these were ever filmed. [Ibid., p. 60.] Apart from *Historia de un gran amor*, she never liked any of the movies made from her screenplays or adapted from her books. Archibaldo Burns directed a film based on two of her short stories—"Perfecto Luna" and "El árbol"—that was released under the title *Juego de mentiras* (Game of Lies); she says that she complained to Burns after watching it: "Oh, Archi, what a lot of foolishness you've added." [Ibid., p. 59.] In 1968, Arturo Ripstein adapted *Recollections of Things to Come*, changing the Cristero War to the Mexican

Revolution. Her response to Ripstein was: "Why was I paid so much for this garbage, man? You could have written it yourselves for nothing." When *Solo de noches vienes* (You Only Come at Night) was made in 1965, with a storyline devised by Elena, Manuel Zeceña, and Sergio Véjar, Elena hated it so much that she wanted her name removed from the credits. Neither did she like *Las puertas del paraíso* (The Gates of Heaven), filmed by Salomón Laiter from a screenplay written by Elena, based on *Reencuentro de personajes*; she was so shocked by the newspaper reviews that she didn't even want to see the movie. In 1958, together with her friend Juan de la Cabada, she wrote the storyline for the successful movie *Las Señoritas Vivanco* (The Vivanco Ladies), starring Sara García and Prudencia Grifell, known as the "grandmothers of Mexican cinema." In regards to that movie, she pronounced, "It was a really funny script, but they handed it over to a woman I was very fond of, a very good, decent, temperate person, but with quite the opposite sense of humor, and she snipped and cut and made it all very discreet and dignified and boring." The woman in question—who, to my mind, had a great sense of humor—was the author and screenwriter Josefina Vicens. I have failed to find any other reference to the relationship between those two huge authors.

Ibid., p. 60.

THE MADRAZO CAUSE

Back in Mexico, Elena began to move in political circles. While on the one hand, she was coming closer to the powers that be—for example, then-Secretary of the Interior, Luis Echeverría, whom she had known since her adolescence when he'd dated her sister—on the other, she continued to help student and activist friends, in addition to sheltering the wounded and taking in those suffering political persecution.

She was also reunited with her high-school friend Carlos Madrazo, who had been governor of Tabasco State and at that time was president of the Institutional Revolutionary Party (PRI). Madrazo was promoting the idea of democratic elections within the party, so that the presidential candidate wouldn't be handpicked by the incumbent, as was then the case, but he came up against such strong opposition that he decided to form a breakaway party, Patria Nueva (PPN). Elena became his ally and confidante. She wrote articles praising him in the magazine *Siempre*, interviewed him, attempted to get his name known outside Mexico. Madrazo invited her to secret meetings and involved her in his plans for the new political party. The energy and passion she'd expended on the defense of campesinos was now dedicated to the Madrazo cause. As a result of this association, she began to receive threats, suffered harassment, and was kept under surveillance. The surviving pages of her 1967 diary (several have been torn out) are a full-blown noir novel, including car chases, frantic escapes, and shootouts.

When asked about her friendship with Madrazo, she responded:

> EG: Yes, Madrazo was so brilliant, so generous, so intelligent. You can't love an idiot. In general, my friends have been intelligent. He had... What's that word that's so fashionable these days?
> RPV: Charisma?
> EG: He was very charismatic. I learned to believe in democracy from him. I didn't use to believe in democracy, but he had such conviction that he got it into my head. Then he died, time has passed, and I don't believe in democracy any longer.

Lectura múltiple, pp. 204-5.

THE ONE ABOUT SPIES

Elena was always making things up, but she also had a very eventful life, and those events were often improbable. On September 30, 1963, she unwillingly agreed to accompany her sister Deva and Helena Paz to a party, complaining that it would be "nothing but communists." Deva was one of the communists. The hostess was Silvia Tirado de Durán, a secretary in the Cuban consulate. Another of the guests was a fair-haired man, a United States citizen whom Elena said was having an affair with Silvia Tirado (who denied the accusation). A few months later, after the assassination of John F. Kennedy, when newspaper images of the assassin appeared, the Elenas recognized the fair-haired man who had danced the Twist in the party as Lee Harvey Oswald. The two of them then went to the Cuban consulate in Mexico to call the diplomats "murderers," among other insults.

Lectura múltiple, p 148.

"Espionage a los intelectuales en los sesenta," (Spying on Intellectuals in the 60s) p. 29.

"La dama misteriosa, Elena Garro y el asesino de Kennedy" (The Mysterious Woman and the Assassination of Kennedy).

Her friend Manuel Calvillo suggested that the Elenas should go into hiding, and they spent a week in the Hotel Vermont. Elena told the story to another friend, the diplomat Charles William Thomas, without being aware that he was a CIA agent who was keeping an eye on her, suspecting her—ironically—of being a communist. Charles set down all this in the "Oswald 201 File." In regards to Garro, he says, "she had a tendency to romanticize developments in reporting on them [which] made it difficult at times to determine what degree of credence to place on what might truly be useful." A year after the assassination, the Elenas went with a CIA agent to declare that they had seen the assassin at a Twist party. Silvia Tirado was detained and interrogated, and it's said that she hated Elena from then on. The CIA eventually decided to dismiss the Elenas' declarations, but a series of documents that were declassified in 2020 support the version that they weren't lying.

"Espionage a los intelectuales en los sesenta," p. 29.

In the same year, the Mexican Federal Security Directorate (DFS) also began to keep Elena under surveillance without her knowledge and to report on her activism.

1968

May 1, 1968

Testimonios sobre Elena Garro, p. 457.

On this date, Elena wrote that the actor Renato Salvatori, in the presence of the actress Susana Dosamantes, told her she should flee, get out, that a lethal trap was being set for her.

July

A movement protesting against state repression sprung up in the principal Mexican universities. It spread and those involved began to question not only that repression, but also the authoritarianism and social and economic policies of Gustavo Díaz Ordaz's government. A student strike was organized and the National Strike Council (CNH) announced a demonstration on August 13.

August 14

Carlos Monsiváis invited Elena Garro and Helena Paz to a session of the Assembly of Intellectuals, Artists, and Writers in the Justo Sierra auditorium of the School of Philosophy and Literature at UNAM.

Monsiváis says of this meeting:

> I'm feeling almost safe when Helena Paz asks to take the floor: "What are we going to do about these events? Students are being killed, they are being imprisoned in the Ministry of the Interior. They have invited us to listen to their complaints and calls, but we haven't been allowed to enter the building. Why isn't a committee being formed to see if they are still being kept prisoners there? I'll tell you why not. The intellectuals are opportunists, self-seekers, they are afraid of losing the cushy jobs they love so much."
>
> What am I supposed to do? Serene, phlegmatic, I realize that I don't have the first idea. The poet Noma Bazúa asks or demands to speak and launches into a diatribe against Elena Garro and Helena Paz. Elena gets to her feet and answers, "I don't know who this lady is and what she says doesn't concern me. I was invited to a meeting of the intelligentsia, but I can see that it's the usual unexceptional characters, arguing and arguing, and by the time they come to a conclusion, the problem has been over for three years. What are you going to do? Or what are we going to do about the unburied dead?"

Debo olvidar, p. 40.

Elena said that on more than one occasion after that meeting, she contributed money to get young people in the movement out of jail and once hid as many as four students. But Madrazo told her not to

Testimonios sobre Elena Garro, p. 273.

Lectura múltiple, p. 152.

sign the manifestos and since she "didn't feel much like signing," she didn't.

One night in August

Sócrates Campos Lemus, one of the leaders of the CNH, came to see Elena. She recounted that he'd appeared at midnight at her home in Lomas de Chapultepec with armed companions and that she was bundled into a car and driven to the outside of the Diana movie theater on Paseo la Reforma. Elena said that Campos Lemus wanted her to use her influence to persuade Madrazo to join the student movement. She agreed to pass on the message but wouldn't intervene personally. She was convinced by what Madrazo had said to her: the movement wasn't going to benefit his presidential candidacy.

Ibid., p. 307.

August 17

Elena published an article in *Revista de América* under the title "El complot de los cobardes" (The Cowards' Plot). In it she claimed that the student movement was being orchestrated by a group of intellectuals, with the aim of influencing the outcome of the 1970 elections, possibly to secure an alliance with the Soviet Union and install a communist dictatorship. According to her, the intellectuals—whom Elena had always dubbed faint-hearted, self-indulgent hypocrites—were manipulating the students, using them as cannon fodder, while they sat comfortably at home, writing.

September 23

Her friend Virgilio Salmerón, a campesino from Oaxaca, told her he'd heard someone say in the Cámara de Diputados that they were going to "fuck her up." The electricity was cut off in her apartment and individuals turned up threatening the domestic staff, who eventually gave in to the harassment and left.

La ingobernable (The Ungovernable Woman), p. 80.

At the end of September, a man named José started to work for her, but the two Elenas decided that he was taking bribes. On the day she burned all the documents she had related to the campesino cause, she locked José in another room. She then took the remaining papers to a female friend for safekeeping. When she returned, José had left, and there were signs that someone else had been in the apartment. Elena said that the telephone rang, she answered, and heard a familiar voice threatening her:

> Is that you, Garro, you bitch? Yes, it's me. Who's speaking? Well, he started hurling insults and telling me what they were going to do to me and how they would kill me and goodness knows what else. I said, Listen, I think it's pretty cowardly to make threats without saying who you are. You know very well who I am, you bastard. Anyway, after that he hung up and I picked up the receiver again to dial the police for help, because I'm no heroine. But the telephone had been cut off, the line was dead. He'd said: We're going to blow up your home. We're here on the corner. So then I told Helena that we were

La cuarta casa.

leaving and, taking nothing but our purses, we ran out. There was a beauty parlor just around the corner and I headed for that. The parlor led to a private residence, and I was taken in there.

September 29
They took refuge at Calle Lisboa 17, in a boarding-house belonging to María Collado, a Spanish widow who had been married to Elena's uncle.

October 2
The CNH organized a public meeting of the student movement in the Plaza de las Tres Culturas. Those assembled were met with gunfire from soldiers and plainclothes police officers. There were hundreds of dead and injured, dozens of people detained, and uncountable disappeared. The international media, who were there to cover the Olympics, reported the massacre, which became a global scandal.

October 4
Octavio Paz handed in his resignation as Ambassador to India in protest at the killings (although, technically, what he did was to request leave of absence and so retain his diplomatic privileges).

October 5 (the same day that Isabel Moncada, the main character in *Recollections*, turns to stone, a coincidence that always troubled Elena).

During a press conference given from the Campo

Militar Número Uno prison, Sócrates Campos Lemus said that, acting on behalf of Madrazo, Elena had offered him money and political support and that they were both seeking to bring down Gustavo Díaz Ordaz's government.

October 6

In the press, it was said that Elena, Carlos Madrazo, and the politician Humberto Romero had organized the student uprising.

Elena recounts that she dialed the number of the "Gobernación" (the Ministry of the Interior). As it was a Sunday, her call was answered by a cleaner, who said there was nobody there. She dialed the Dirección Federal de Seguridad (the former intelligence agency, known as the DFS) and another cleaner said the same thing. After that, she called Carlos Madrazo, who proposed that she talk to the press first.

Debo olvidar, p. 16.

Helena Paz sent María Collado's assistant out to buy Miss Clairol and they both dyed their hair black.

While one of the boarding-house guests, by the surname of Echauri, was advising them to attack Sócrates, the phone rang. A voice threatened to blow up the house where "those two bitches" were staying.

Ibid.

María ordered the mother and daughter to leave. They ignored her.

Helena Paz called the editorial office of *Novedades*, telling them to send a reporter. Elena said that Sócrates was lying and asked for a face-to-face meeting with him.

The journalist departed and the Spanish guests left

the boardinghouse, fearing they might be deported.

The Elenas called the editorial offices of all the city newspapers. Reporters arrived from *El Universal, Excélsoir*, and *La Prensa*, among others. Óscar del Rivero, from *El Universal*, quoted her as saying, "The students aren't responsible for the discontent with president Díaz Ordaz's government; it's a group of over five hundred Mexican and foreign intellectuals, the majority protected by their senior positions in the Universidad Autónoma de México and the Politécnico." And also, "Those far-left intellectuals sent the students out on a crazy escapade that has cost lives and caused sorrow in many Mexican homes."

Diálogos con Elena Garro, p. 325.

Ibid., p. 237.

Del Rivero quotes several names: Luis Villoro, Jesús Silva Herzog, José Luis Cuevas, Leonora Carrington, Ricardo Guerra, Carlos Monsiváis, and others. Although she discredits the movement, in her declarations, Elena admits to having had contact with the students, to having received them in her home and to protecting and hiding more than one injured person. In one particular paragraph of the article, she uses the plural, including herself in the "intellectuals" when she says, "On seeing the awful consequences of the events in Nonoalco Tlatelolco, I spoke to some of them, asking that we accept responsibility for the hundreds of detained youths and turn ourselves in to the Attorney General's Office, but none of them were willing to do that."

Ibid.

Elena always claimed that she didn't give the names of any of those "five hundred intellectuals." When asked who was behind the movement, she stated that the responsibility lay with the people who had marched and signed the declarations. "The intellectuals signed many manifestos, I didn't. That's where their names are."

Ibid., p. 323.

When she'd finished her declarations, Elena phoned the Gobernación and the DFS, telling them to come and arrest her. She dialed the numbers there, in front of the journalists: "Elena Garro speaking. I insist that you come to detain me. You can put me before a firing squad if I'm guilty."

Ibid., p. 322.

When the reporters left, María Collado again asked the Elenas to leave the boardinghouse. They refused.

At that point a soldier knocked at the door. A Captain Salazar ordered them to remain in the boardinghouse and offered Elena his pistol to protect herself. Elena refused, saying, "You need it more than I do. You only have the whole army and the police on your side." Before leaving, Salazar added, "Señora, make your escape. There's no hope for you."

Debo olvidar, p. 23.

October 7

Elena appeared on the front pages of the newspapers; "Elena Garro Blames 500 Intellectuals," read the headline in *El Universal*. They also published cartoons mocking her.

In another press conference, Carlos Madrazo refuted Sócrates's declarations. He didn't mention Elena Garro but declared that he had at no time had contact with the movement and would never have been persuaded "to collaborate in causing a confrontation

Diálogos con Elena Garro, p. 320.

between the youth and the army."

The best and most detailed narrative of what happened after that day can be found in the book *Debo olvidar que existí* (I Must Forget I Existed) by Rafael Cabrera. In it, he recounts that when the international press arrived at María Collado's home, Elena reiterated that she wasn't behind the movement. After that, two agents of the DFS—Soberón and Mayorga—turned up and took her into custody. When she asked why they were taking her away, they replied that it was for her own safety; the communists wanted her dead.

Debo olvidar, p. 26-9.

She was driven to the headquarters of the DFS and taken to the office of Fernando Gutiérrez Barrios, a person Elena knew and admired. He laughed at the sight of her dyed hair.

María Collado insisted that Helena Paz leave. Some of her friends came to collect her and attempted to hide her in the Miguel Alemán apartment complex, near the university, but after the killings in Tlatelolco, the building was surrounded by police. They then took her to the house of her paternal grandmother, who refused to let the "brazen communist" in. She was finally driven to the Gobernación, where Helena asked to be detained with her mother. They agreed. On the way, a stop was made at Elena's apartment to pick up their dog, cats, and a few clothes. The animals were left in the care of María Collado. Mother and daughter were then transferred together to the DFS, and later to the Hotel Casa Blanca.

Ibid., p. 80.

October 22

From the hotel, where they were kept in isolation and under constant surveillance—by a man they called "The Turtle" and other agents—Elena sent a telegram to Bioy Casares, asking him to collect signatures from Argentinian authors to send a message of support for her to the Mexican government. He and Borges signed, Silvina Ocampo preferred not to. Helena Paz would later say that they were drugged with barbiturates in the hotel. According to Elena, she was constantly pressured to make a declaration against Madrazo but never gave way. She also said that she threatened to kill herself so they would let the two of them out.

Elena Garro: los recuerdos sin porvenir, p. 88.

Lectura múltiple, pp. 305-6.

October 23

A newspaper published a letter from Helena Paz to her father, reprimanding him for his role, along with the "intellectuals," in the October 2 tragedy. Helena identified the guilty parties as Monsiváis, Rosario Castellanos, Luis Villoro, and Octavio Paz himself. She later said that she stood by her declaration and that she'd written the letter partly because that was her opinion, and partly from fear of what might happen to them. She also made a note of President Gustavo Díaz Ordaz's words to her: "See here, Helenita, based on the reports from Gutiérrez Barrios and Echeverría, I'd have given your mamacita thirty years if it hadn't been for that letter." The DFS itself sent the letter to *El Universal* and the Gobernación paid for it to be translated and published in English and French.

Debo olvidar, p. 80.

November 29

They returned to María Collado's boardinghouse, staying in a room with restricted telephone access, kept under surveillance by Fernando Gutiérrez Barrios and two agents. The intellectuals were by then responding to Elena's declaration: Carlos Monsiváis called her "the singer of the year," and the painter José Luis Cuevas said she'd suffered "a sudden attack of madness." To this, Elena would say decades later:

Lectura múltiple, p. 212.

> I was afraid and fear can lead you to say and do outlandish things. If I said the rector (Javier Barros Sierra) was very much to blame for having thrown the young people into the street, Cuevas is right when he says I suffered a sudden attack of madness brought on by panic, but an attack of madness, nonetheless. I must have spoken those words, but I ask the rector's forgiveness for them. I never bore a grudge against Cuevas for what he said about my sudden attack; it really made me laugh and still does. Hell, I still remember how shocked I was that morning! It's printed like a photo in my memory. But fear stalked the city…

1969

January 15
Her dog, Agripina, died, probably poisoned.

January 16
Helena Paz adopted two cats.

January 20
The cats died, probably poisoned. Elena narrated that second stay in María Collado's boardinghouse in *Sócrates y los gatos*.

January 22
They left the boardinghouse. From that moment on, they were fugitives:

> I fled to a friend's house, but she wouldn't let me in. Another friend wouldn't let me in either. Then I went to a nephew's house; he wasn't home but a niece let me in. I stayed there for a few days and began to notice that the Federals were hanging around. So then I went back to

Lectura múltiple, pp. 309-10.

> the DFS. I said, "You might as well just get it done with and kill me properly, not hunt me like a rat in the street." They took me from there to another hotel and, one day, I went out and didn't return. I took refuge in a convent in [Colonia] Florida.

June 4

Debo olvidar, p. 148.

Carlos Madrazo died on Mexicana de Aviación flight 704. His death was put down as an accident; the plane crashed into the Tres Pico hillside in Serranía del Fraile. Witnesses on the ground said the plane exploded before it crashed. Elena's nephew and niece suggested hiding her with a woman named Carmela, in a house on the outskirts of the city. When they arrived there, Carmela was high on drugs and attempted to stab Elena. They got out of there fast.

Testimonios sobre Elena Garro, p. 405.

According to a retrospective entry in her diary, before Madrazo's funeral, Elena received a call from Gutiérrez Barrios who—assuming that she would organize the event—ordered her to be prudent and not to hold a large gathering for the burial. Her friend César Tosca saw her crying and confirmed that Madrazo had been assassinated, that Che Guevara's former secretary had explained how the plane in which he was killed had been sabotaged.

Few people attended the vigil. When they left the funeral parlor that night in a cab, a black car without plates followed them. Elena asked the driver to stop near the Hotel de México to throw off their pursuers. Men carrying pistols got out of the black car. Helena

Paz tried to get out but Elena told her to stay where she was and they returned to the funeral parlor. The director confirmed that Madrazo had been killed by a bomb and said that the only remains were shreds of skin and fragments of bone. He hid the Elenas in the corpse freezer, where they spent the night among the dead. When the funeral procession arrived, they escaped through the back door.

Summer

Despite having no money, they stayed in a number of hotels in the north of the country; some good Samaritans came to their aid, drove them, and covered their expenses.

> I was handed the bill, they handed it to me and I didn't [pay]. One day the manager called me and said, "You're Elenita Garro, right?" I said I was. "And you can't afford to pay the tab?" "No, I have no money." "Don't worry, I'm a Madracista too. Stay as long as you like." And I did.

Lectura múltiple, pp. 309-10.

They adopted two new cats: Serafín and Úrsula, who got lost on the train when they were returning to Mexico City. On a couple of occasions, Elena made note of phone calls to Gutiérrez Barrios, in which he seems to have told her not to come back to the capital. She also wrote that Gutiérrez Barrios's agents had found them in a hotel in Torreón; they managed to escape and reached El Paso, Texas.

Debo olvidar, pp. 153-60.

From there they traveled to New York but returned

to Mexico soon afterward. When things calmed a little and they were able to find the money, they moved to an apartment in Polanco, at Calle Taine 220, where they lived until 1972.

1972

Ibid., p. 177.

One day, Raúl Urgellés—a student and friend of Elena's—visited her and said he'd heard rumors that she was going to be assassinated. This news coincided with Helena Paz's diagnosis of cancer, and Roberto Garza, their friend and doctor, advised Elena to "get la Chatita out of Mexico; even the operating table isn't free of politics."

La cuarta casa.

SEPTEMBER 29, 1972

On the feast day of her beloved St. Michael the Archangel (when, four years before, they'd had to escape a bomb threat), they crossed the border into the United States. Elena said that their passports had been confiscated so they had to cross as undocumented migrants. In her diary, she noted that the driver who took them across the desert got lost near Cerro del Fraile, where her friend Madrazo had died, and when a tire blew out, Moreno—the driver—and Elena changed it together. To ease their fears in the darkness of the desert, Moreno asked Elena to sing something and she began with Mexican songs. She'd assumed that Moreno didn't know her name, but she saw that he had a copy of *Recollections of Things to Come* on the front seat and had recognized her from the author photo. At the border, they were met by a soldier with orders to wave them through, and they crossed without problems.

Testimonios sobre Elena Garro, p. 358.

SOUND AND FURY

1968 marks Elena's expulsion from the heights of the elite. Her descent from Olympus. It is a fundamental year for her, the dramatic climax of her life, and I carefully read and reread everything I could find about that whole situation, but I still didn't understand what the hell happened. I tried to exercise patience; told myself it was just a matter of being more organized, filling out index cards, making lists, chronologies. But however hard I tried, however close I got, stepped back, turned it all over again, I still didn't understand. I'd been looking for a detective story in that period of her life and instead I found a mix of random chance, violence, chaos, intrigue, poor decisions, and lousy luck. As Shakespeare would say, a tale full of sound and fury.

FURTHER REFLECTIONS

In 1968, my paternal grandfather, Alfredo Barrera—the son of that great-grandfather who worked with Paz in Yucatán—was director of the Natural History Museum in Mexico City. My grandmother, Isabel Bassols, the daughter of my other great-grandparents—the ones who appear in the photo, dining and chatting with Elena and Paz—was teaching at the Instituto Politécnico Nacional and got involved in the student movement.

My father was only seven at the time, but he clearly remembers that on October 1, the day before the massacre, when he was walking home, he saw tanks and convoys of troops passing. On the preceding nights, his parents had discussed the latest news and rumors about the movement. His older brothers and sisters were already in high school and were involved in the protests. Isabel spent the whole of the day before the massacre on the telephone to her mother and siblings. That night, when Alfredo sat down to dinner, he ordered that nobody—not my aunts, uncles, or grandmother—was to attend the gathering in

Tlatelolco the next day. "Something is going to happen," he said. On October 2, my father walked home from school with a friend, the son of one of the leaders of the movement, who had been staying with them for a day or two, probably—my father thinks—because his family lived in Tlatelolco. When they reached home, Isabel wasn't there. She'd left everything ready for the day's meal but had defied her husband's instructions and had gone to Tlatelolco with her sister Aurelia.

The two of them were at the demonstration, listening to a speech when the shooting broke out. They ran, were separated; Isabel hid in a store with some other people, huddled behind a safe, which received a number of bullets. During a pause in the shooting they lowered the store's metal grate, but the soldiers eventually found them and made them all line up outside, with bullets whizzing around them. Isabel heard other people in the line behind her fall; I'm not sure how she managed to get out of that situation, but after a while she went to look for Aurelia at the house of her mother, Clementina, who lived nearby.

While this was going on my grandfather got home unusually early. As a government employee—the museum is a government institution—he had privileged information about what was going to happen that day. He was nervous, sweating, looking around in confusion as though unsure where he was. He poured himself a shot of tequila, as he did every evening, but was so tense that the glass broke in his hand. When the children saw the bleeding wound, they ran to try to help him, but he told them to stay there in the house and got into the car to go in search of Isabel. When he arrived in Tlatelolco, the soldiers pulled him out of his vehicle and he was loaded into a truck. Someone got in and asked all those detained there to show their identification. Alfredo took out his museum credentials and was allowed to leave. He searched for his wife a while longer without success and got back home devastated. And there was Isabel, safe and sound. Her sister was also unharmed.

My father remembers that when they went to Tlalelolco the following day to recover the car, they found it with many other vehicles that were covered in bullet holes, but my grandfather's car was, inexplicably, intact. They were about to leave when they heard more shooting coming from the tops of buildings.

After October 2, as the political tensions began to die down, Alfredo left the country on his own for several months. Things were never the same in my family, or in the families of thousands of other Mexicans after that day.

ASTRAL CHART

In *Protagonistas de la literatura mexicana*, Elena analyzes her daughter's character based on her zodiac sign. Helena was Sagittarius, and according to Elena, that means she was "the traveler, adventurer, and clown of the zodiac." She says that her ascendent in Gemini gives her a "dual personality, makes her cerebral, intellectual, and intelligent." The conjunction of Moon–Venus in her natal chart made her "a glamor girl, a lover of the moon, beauty parlors, perfumes, ponds, lakes, pastel colors, silks, and poetry." Jupiter and Mars in the Tenth House foretold "a great military career." Neptune in the Fourth House suggested:

Protagonistas, p. 494.

> One or both of her parents is peculiar. Neptune is "afflicted" and that affliction produces confused familial relationships in a chaotic family environment. This aspect of Neptune gives rise to family secrets in the birth house and "skeletons in the closet." It also indicates that the subject loves to live near water. The position of Uranus shows political exile and banishment.

Ibid., p. 495.

To follow up on my "divinations" about the past, I decided to consult an astrologer named Dominique and asked her to read the astral birth chart of Elena Garro, also a Sagittarius. She has spent a few days studying the material and is now here with me.

She explains that Elena had her ascendent in Leo, with the moon in Cancer. Her astral chart shows a predominance of fire and a lack of air, which represents rational aspects. The consequence of this can be problems with objectivity and perception, but at the same time a very sharp intellect. Neither Tolstoy, Dumas, nor Hemingway had air in their chart, says Dominique, nor did Marlon Brando.

Elena's chart shows dissatisfaction and difficult, problematic relationships. The ascendent has a very strong influence on the most evident characteristics; as Leo rules the Sun, there's something very solar about her. The need to achieve power, exercise authority, and express herself creatively are some of the characteristics of Leo. They can also be exhibitionists, generous, extravagant, and proud. For Dominique, it is clear that the relationship with Paz was not a smooth one: he was Aries with his ascendent in Sagittarius. The two of them spoke the language of fire. And to cap it all off, Paz had Pluto in the Seventh House, the house of marriage! Pluto, she tells me, brings out the worst in people. Elena would have needed a partner with a water sign.

There is, Dominique says, something infantile in the chart. People with the sign of Sagittarius are like that, a bit childish—they often feel superior. They are also adventurous and like travel; they enjoy knowing other worlds. Her Moon in cancer makes her empathetic, emotional, unstable, moody, bountiful, and protective. She has Jupiter in the Ninth House, something that is common in politicians and writers. Mercury is in opposition to Pluto, which means she never accepts things at their face value, is very suspicious, and has a detective mind. That's why she's also attracted to anything secret, mysterious, and esoteric. And that's undoubtedly why she liked tarot and horoscopes.

BETTER THAN POETS

An entire book could be written about Elena's relationship to animals in general and cats in particular. When she was a child, her grandfather, Tranquilino, used to call her "Leona." She became a vegetarian as a teenager and said that Paz used to berate her for it, telling her that Hitler was vegetarian. One of the worst fights Elena had with Paz's mother was because—as she says in her diary and in interviews—her mother-in-law killed Moshi Moshi, the cat Elena had brought back from Japan. Paz insisted that their new apartment in Mexico City was too small to house an animal as well, so the cat was given to his mother, who hung it from a peach tree one day. Elena said it was such a smart cat that it learned to use the toilets on the ship from Japan to Mexico and liked to be thrown breadcrumb balls.

Memorias de España 1937, loc. 792.

Andamos huyendo, Lola, p. 322.

Testimonios sobre Elena Garro, pp. 206-8.

Elena Garro's cats always accompanied her in her wanderings. Some of them were famous; for example, Humitos Madrazo—named after her friend Carlos Madrazo—and Úrsula and Serafín, two cats she lost that became characters in her books. And there were also Petrouchka and Lola, who gave her name to one of the protagonists of *Andamos huyendo, Lola*. Episodes in that book are narrated from the viewpoint of cats, and, when not, the narrator describes their attitudes, feelings, and thoughts with the same attention to detail devoted to the human characters. Elena wrote an elegy to Lola that says, "How am I going to sleep / if you don't jump up onto my bed?"

Cristales de tiempo, p. 239.

The Elenas took two cats with them to the boardinghouse they moved to following the Tlatelolco massacre, but they later fled when someone poisoned their pets. Based on that event, Elena wrote the play *Sócrates y los gatos*, in which one of the characters says, "I think that I am them [the cats] or that they sacrificed themselves for us. I don't know...You said Humitos was your double or your other self..."

Teatro completo, p. 333.

During the months lived in hiding following the 1968 debacle, they still managed to adopt cats. When they took flight again and didn't know what to do with the animals, Elena decided to send Maxi, Lafitte, Ana María, and Tony to Argentina, where Bioy Casares lived very comfortably. Bioy accepted them, but Silvina, who was a dog- rather than cat-person, had them sent to a cattery. Bioy told Elena that he'd taken them to their house in the country, but even that white lie seemed to her a betrayal. In interviews, she said that was the moment she fell out of love with Bioy. Twenty years of loving, when not passionate, correspondence ended on the spot.

La Hermana menor (The Younger Sister), p. 102.

In a chapter of *Andamos huyendo, Lola* called "Las cuatro moscas" (The Four Flies), the protagonist plays at being a fly, and in one of the stories in *La semana de colores* ("El día que fuimos perros"), the characters pretend to be dogs for a day. Elena also had dogs she was very fond of, and they appear in other works she wrote; for instance, in *Andamos huyendo*, there's an episode where Lelinca reports a man for mistreating his dog. But there are more cats than dogs and flies in her life and works (or so I believe, even though nobody ever counts how many flies there are in the world).

While living in exile in New York, the Elenas procured Lola and Petrouchka, and these two cats eventually traveled with them to Spain. They had to hide them when staying in hotels and were often asked to leave when their presence was discovered.

Lectura múltiple, p. 158.

When Elena finally returned to Mexico in 1993, the state exempted her from paying taxes on the thirteen cats she brought with her. The tiny apartment in Cuernavaca where she spent her last years was completely overrun by them. She could tell all thirteen apart by their meows.

Ibid.

She said that cats were better than poets: "They're divine, their every movement is poetic, and, unlike poets, they have no interest in earning money or being awarded grants for it."

Poniatowska, *Obras reunidas*, p. 97.

Her manuscripts, diaries, and letters have many brownish stains and, even today, smell strongly of cat piss.

In those diaries, it is animals that cause her to doubt her Catholicism and the existence of God. An example of this is when she writes that her cat Güendolina had four kittens, three strawberry blond and one white, but one of them, Mario-María, died tragically just days after being born. "These things test my belief in God. How can he allow it?" And then she goes on, "I've never liked that part of the Catholic faith that says animals can't enter heaven. So where do they go? It's just human arrogance."

Testimonios sobre Elena Garro, p. 476.

"I'm only interested in the fate of animals and only see myself reflected in them," she says in a letter to José Bianco.

José Bianco Papers.

"The heaven that awaits me is in the eyes of animals," is a phrase from her play *Parada San Ángel* that I repeat here because I find it so beautiful.

Teatro completo, p. 390.

PUTTING WORDS TOGETHER

Becoming a writer was never Elena's Plan A, not even B or C. "I wanted to be a ballerina or a general," she told Emmanuel Carballo. "The idea of sitting down to write instead of reading seemed ridiculous." Reading was her passion, which is why her father encouraged her to write.

Protagonistas, p. 477.

Writing, however, sprung from the same source as theater and dance: an intimate but extensive landscape that she described in the following way: "The only freedom I believe in exists within an open space inside ourselves, the only free space left to us in which to dream, think, and create."

Teatro completo, p. xxxiii.

And she dedicated herself to writing in all its genres. She wrote poetry (for several years on the sly; she said Paz prohibited that activity and made her either burn her poems or rewrote them himself if he liked the idea, then signed them as his own), plays, novels, short stories, and essays, and reflected a great deal on language and writing.

Elena Garro: los recuerdos sin porvenir, p. 94.

In the play *La dama Boba* (The Foolish Lady), she describes the performative quality of language as an

Teatro completo, p. 144.

instrument for seeing in the dark: "It's getting dark, this isn't the time for talk…Giving a name to darkening is what darkens, but if you don't name things at night, you can't see anything. (Blackout)."

She also understands writing as a game (sometimes a dangerous one). In the poem "Reproches a mi lengua" (Reproaches to My Tongue), she says:

Cristales de tiempo, p. 124.

> Tiger, playing ball with the words.
> Words you take from my mouth!
> And you deepen the wounds
> with your claws, sharp
> as vinegar.

Protagonistas, p. 468.

For her, writing was also a form of amusement and a job like any other: "I have the impression that I'm writing for nobody. But if I don't write, how am I going to kill time? And anyway, there have been days when I wouldn't have eaten without it."

José Bianco Papers.

She called it the profession of "putting words together." The writers she didn't like were "word-gluers," and in a letter to José Bianco, she said, "Putting words together: dizzying."

She was aware also of the political and ethical aspects of language, its redemptive power, and the need for words to be spoken aloud, for the words *truth*, *dialogue*, and *justice*, and the risk involved in taking responsibility for them. In *Felipe Ángeles,* the protagonist says:

Teatro completo, p. 233.

> I don't know if anybody has heard me, but I do know that you have to speak out in this

> cemetery you've made of the country, a place where there's nothing to hear but screams and gunfire. I'm aware that speaking out here is the most serious of crimes; here where terror has reduced men to babbling. But, General, I won't give up my humanity. And humans are language. And listen carefully, General Escobar, all I want is for everyone to speak, for men's voices to be heard instead of men drowning in blood. You have to speak, General, even if it costs your life. You have to name the tyrants, their welts, their murders, the dead, the wretched, to free them from their wretchedness. Man is freed by words.

She also recognized the danger of lying and traitorous words. Again, in "Reproches a mi lengua," she says:

> This language that sleeps in my mouth
> Selfish cat that never says a true word!
> This dagger-language that kills what I love
> dagger that betrays me, wounds me
> sword that unleashes tempests

Cristales de tiempo, p. 124.

José Cariño, the endearing character and Ixtepec's best madman in *Recollections of Things to Come*, is an advocate of dictionaries: "words were dangerous because they had an existence of their own and the defense of dictionaries prevented unimaginable catastrophes." Every day, he goes out to pick up the evil

Recollections, p. 55.

words that escape from the dictionary, words like *to hang* and *to torture*, and returns them to the dictionary before they can do any more harm.

THE LOSS OF THE KINGDOM

In New York, 1972, she read José Bianco's *La perdida del reino*, loosely based on the youthful experiences of their group of friends in Paris. After finishing the novel, she told Pepe Bianco, "I was already downhearted, but your book finished me off. And why must one go on living when one no longer believes in the world? The gossip column genre is frightful and I've been dragged into it with a grand fanfare. Disgusting! I've seriously thought of suicide."

José Bianco Papers.

She also told Pepe that she was rewriting (patching up, she put it) the last part of *Testimonios sobre Mariana*, which also takes inspiration from those shared times in Paris: "There we are, all together again, but very different from the way we appear in *La pérdida del reino*. I'm worse than you and we're both like veritable garbage or monsters."

Ibid.

During that time in the United States, the Elenas lived for a few months in a house on the coast, but they were finally forced to move out after a falling out with the owner and a neighbor, whom, in her diaries, Elena calls "the pallid Dracula" or "the Transylvanian."

Paz was still annoyed with them about the 1968 letter. Elena's diaries say that he initially refused to visit his daughter when she had her operation, wouldn't pay the hospital bills or talk to her on the phone. But he later reappeared, contacted Helena Paz's medical team, and began to pay for and oversee her treatment. Helena Paz's poor health was no secret; she spent large amounts of time in her bed, had crippling hemorrhages, and sometimes coughed up blood.

Testimonios sobre Elena Garro, pp. 346 and 393.

Elena was constantly worrying about her financial situation, yet she continued to spend what little she had on luxury items and extravagances. "I overspent on December 24: armchairs, the dinner, white lace curtains, turrón, etc. At the last minute, I dashed out with Martín to get glasses, plates, and a shelf. Now I've got three dollars to my name," she writes in her diary.

Ibid., p. 341.

In New York, she also continued to receive news of the assassinations of other friends. Her diary entries following the threats of death, bombing, and torture show that she developed a fear of telephones, which seemed to her like dangerous animals, to be avoided at all costs.

During that time in the United States, she became obsessed with a person she referred to as "La Giganta." The real name of that giant was June Cobb, who really had worked with Fidel Castro and had later been a CIA informant. According to Elena, La Giganta once stayed with her in Mexico and threw her cat out the window at midnight. In New York, Cobb said she wanted to help her and handed over some delayed letters from Eunice Odio—the poet who, from Mexico, was trying

Elena Garro Papers.

to handle Elena's return, mediating with Paz and Luis Echeverría. La Giganta also brought her Jell-Os every day, which seemed sinister to Elena. Then, one day, Elena called Eunice Odio and the police answered. She hung up. La Giganta, Elena claimed, tricked her into going to Immigration and had her phone cut off, then she told her that Eunice had been beaten to death and Elena—who tended to be egocentric in such (and other) matters—thought it was because Eunice hadn't managed to persuade her to return to Mexico. Echeverría asked her to come back, but Elena foresaw a lugubrious future for herself there and stayed where she was. Other friends in Mexico advised her not to return. As their passports had expired months before, they were in danger of being deported back to Mexico but, without saying anything to Cobb, Elena managed to get a bureaucrat to take pity on her and her daughter and issue them with new ones.

TWO THOUGHTS ON EXILE

Lectura múltiple, p. 201.

"As human beings, wherever we go, we'll always be the same because defeat is carried inside yourself. A change of place changes nothing."

Ibid., p. 238.

"I believe that separating yourself from everything is Hell...I believe that exile is a mistake because it's living in a vacuum, there is absolutely no echo, exile is a little wretched."

THE ONE ABOUT SHOCKS

In her diaries and letters there is no shortage of words like "faggot" and "ladyboy." If she'd been born forty or fifty years later, would she have used such expressions? I like to think not, but there's no way of knowing for sure. On a number of occasions, Elena publicly insinuated and openly declared in her diaries and in conversation that Archibaldo Burns and Octavio Paz were homosexuals. She calls them "fags" and terms the power they exercise the "homocracy." Laura Ramos remembers her saying, about Paz, that "he liked young men and old ones too…poets…all of them. Before we met and on our first trip to Spain, he tried all that out; later he'd humiliate me and make me do it that way." Homophobic ideas were common currency in those days. And Octavio Paz himself wrote to Elena from Berkeley about the rumor that his roommate was homosexual: "All that about Bravo disgusts me: I haven't noticed anything, besides his being a bit of an oddball." But on the other hand, both Paz and Elena Garro had good friends who were homosexual.

Elena Garro: Recuerdos sin porvenir, p. 62.

Odi et amo, p. 406.

Elena wrote many stories strongly criticizing class

prejudice in Mexico, and yet she was capable of being shockingly classist herself. For instance, one day in New York, a man told her that feeding the pigeons wasn't allowed and she should pick up the crumbs she'd scattered. Elena recognized his Latin American accent and, furious, shouted, "Filthy Indian, take your hands off me and vacuum up the trash with your snout, that's what you're paid for."

Elena Garro Papers.

THE CATS ARE UNHAPPY

On May 29, 1974, Elena and her daughter flew from New York to Spain. They initially stayed with family members, but soon there were disagreements with them too—the episode inspired her novella *La casa junto al río* (The House by the River), in which a woman discovers a band of murderers among her extended family, trying to get their hands on her inheritance. She writes lists in her diary of all the hotels they stayed in, speaks of the cold and hunger, of how hard it was to make ends meet. There were days when they didn't eat and at one point they ended up in a homeless shelter, where they could spend the night but had to leave during the day: "I'm in a shelter for beggars… Helenita asked for a job at the Embassy and was sent to a doctor, who diagnosed malnutrition, anemia, very low blood pressure, danger of cardiac arrest, in short: hunger."

Lectura múltiple, p. 24.

Octavio Paz sent 400 dollars a month, although in several diary entries, Elena complains that the payments were late or never made, and that she couldn't afford Helenita's medical expenses; she was still suffering hemorrhages. They were regularly threatened with having the electricity, water, and phone cut off and often had to skip out by moonlight from hotels. Elena couldn't find work. They suffered from lack of money, but when they had even a little, they would splurge on new clothes and meals in the best seafood restaurants. In addition, Elena sometimes gave money and food to a woman named Eulalia, who was poorer than them and had a young son.

Testimonios sobre Elena Garro, p. 427.

Elena's mother, Esperanza Navarro, died on June 29, 1976. "Deep, deep depression," says her diary. The Elenas didn't leave their beds for days at a time.

She started to elaborate ludicrous theories, like the one that Hitler was a former communist agent. Fear added to depression turned the Elenas into chronic invalids: they suffered from agoraphobia and persecution mania. When they went outdoors, they were convinced that emissaries sent by Octavio Paz were following them in the street and taking photographs. Elena began writing her diary in English so nobody could read it (or maybe it was pure vanity).

At one point, their neighbors made a formal complaint about the noise they made at night, with people coming and going at all hours. The Elenas were visited in succession by a man Elena nicknamed "the Magus," another she called "the Crocodile," and a woman who was "the Huge Spider."

Ibid., p. 400.

Writing wasn't easy. "I'll never find a place where I can read or write," she says in her diary. "I'm condemned to not writing." Lack of money led her to pawn her typewriter and there was a time when she had no books to read or glasses to read them with. But one day, out of the blue, she succeeded in working on *Testiminios sobre Mariana*. "I'm exhausted. I just want to write, write, and write," says her diary. She began to dust off old manuscripts in order to publish anything that would earn her a little money.

Ibid., p. 434.

Here are some entries in her diary between 1975 and 1976:

> "We don't go out. Wake up feeling harrowed."
> "What are we going to do? We have no money."
> "Woke feeling depressed."
> "[Helena] confessed that she wanted to go to the pharmacy alone because she's afraid of going to the pharmacy alone and wants to overcome her fear. I confessed that I was also suffering agoraphobia."
> "In the middle of the plaza, where the monument is, I was suddenly terrified. I couldn't take a step forward. I thought I was going mad."
> "We haven't had a bite to eat all day."
> "Helenita is deeply depressed."
> "Very little to eat. The cats were unhappy."

Elena Garro Papers.

The only cheerful entry in her diary during those years seems to be the day they went to the Prado. They thought the museum "lovely, lovely, lovely."

Testimonios sobre Elena Garro, p. 361.

She had to put up a fight to get a Spanish passport, but she finally succeeded and, on Franco's death, Enrique Tierno Galván, the socialist mayor of Madrid, set them up in an apartment.

ONEIRIC BABIES

One night, in my horrible hotel in Princeton, I dream that someone puts a dark-haired baby girl in my arms. The baby is Elena Garro. How can this be the famous Elena Garro? I think in the dream. How could a baby have written all those books? And wasn't she fair-haired? Except for the white mane of her later years and the time she dyed her hair black in 1968, Elena was blonde. It's said that even as she aged, she was still naturally blonde. At times she seemed to really like that distinctive physical trait that boosted her status in a racist society. Yet, in parallel, at certain points, it was one more trait that set her apart, impeded her from belonging, made her stranger, a foreigner: "Too bad we don't have black braids!" says a blonde child in the short story "La semana de colores."

The Week of Colors, p. 71.

"It's her, it's her," someone says to me in the dream. I know the baby is Elena, but I have no idea how I'm going to care for her.

Weeks later, I read in her diary entry for July 11, 1973, that, while taking a siesta, Elena dreamed that she had a naked baby boy in her arms. "I went into a movie theater and there he was on the huge screen, with his head escaping from the edge of the screen. 'How strange, it's the same child as I have in my arms,' I thought." The baby tells her that its mother is with its siblings and Elena doesn't understand how such a little baby can speak so well.

Testimonios sobre Elena Garro, p. 318.

THE CONSOLATION OF THE TAROT

Tarot is a constant presence in her exile diaries. Possibly due to the influence of her theosophical father, Elena was accustomed to doing tarot readings, casting the *I Ching*, palm reading, and making astral birth charts. Given the uncertainty surrounding the Elenas' lives, tarot was a comfort, almost always corroborating their misfortunes and attributing them to a destiny over which they had no control. And that was what the cards usually predicted: misfortune: "Awful tarot"; "I woke up in anguish and laid out a tarot. Awful"; "Awful tarot"; "I woke feeling very anxious. Between them, the horoscope, Chata, tarot, and Transylvania have left me terrified"; "Despair: I laid out a tarot. Center Ten of Wands against the Moon, past the Tower reversed. Future, the Devil. Above Strength reversed. Reason: Temperance. Fear of Death reversed, Coming to me, Justice. Hidden Desire. Reversed Lovers. End Wheel of Fortune. I should be totally without hope."

Testimonios sobre Elena Garro, pp. 319, 333, 320, 321, and 327.

There are only a couple of occasions in her diaries when tarot readings brought good news, but then she loses confidence in them: "We ask if Federico

Ibid., p. 316.

is going to call and if the engineer will show a little charity, it seems both will happen but tarot sometimes gets it wrong." Vilma Fuentes, who was a close friend of Elena's during her last stay in Paris, says that they sometimes even asked the cards if the cards were telling the truth.

Elena Garro: la pérdida del reino, p. 71.

People visited them regularly to have their tarots and astral charts read. In her diary, Elena complains that it's the only reason they come. The two Elenas lay out the spread for someone named Mercedes, a certain Mary Carmen, and a pair of strangers; they read the horoscope of an Antonio and would sometimes stay up until four or five in the morning, dealing cards for their friends. The neighbors continue complaining about the noise during the night. In one diary entry, Elena recounts the visit of a certain Enrique, who tells her that somebody else read his tarot and the Queen of Swords came out in reverse. Enrique was convinced that the Queen of Swords was Elena.

Testimonios sobre Elena Garro, p. 388.

In an interview, Lucía Melgar asks:

> LM: Have you ever had your cards read?
> EG: No. Well, Helena has read them for me! She's a fervent believer in tarot.
> LM: How did the reading come out?
> EG: Well, we laid them out so often it didn't work… Have you had your tarot read?
> LM: I don't really do that sort of thing.
> EG: I do, but [one day when] we were in Paris, a priest said tarot was playing with the Devil and black magic. I said, "Oh, how dreadful!" And I

Lectura múltiple, pp. 293-4.

gathered up all the packs Helena had—she collected them—and burned them. I didn't want anything to do with black magic in the house. Because it does exist. I was frightened.

Testimonios sobre Elena Garro, p. 423.

"Only tarot consoles me," says one of her diary entries.

INCORRIGIBLE

"Why do you want to do a reading for Elena Garro?" asks Julián Herbert. We're at the Oaxaca Book Fair and he has his tarot deck with him at all times. We've just been involved in an event to launch a book about the impossible task of copyediting a manuscript, and before it started, he'd drawn out three cards to see what direction the discussion should take. I didn't manage to get a glimpse of which cards he drew and have no idea what they said to him, but I guess they gave good advice because our conversation flowed easily and we laughed a lot. I told him that I've been trying to edit this book, and that it seems to me like Elena Garro herself; incorrigible, beyond repair.

We're sitting at a table on the terrace, and I tell Julián that I've always been pretty skeptical about such things, but that suddenly it seems like a great idea to read Elena Garro's cards. I'm getting desperate. After months of research, of reading her books, her correspondence, her diaries, and several biographies, there are still many things I don't understand. Too many. And I don't know what else I can do, where to look for answers. But Elena liked tarot, so it seems to make sense to try there. Is that possible? I ask Julián. Is it possible to do a reading for Elena Garro?

Julián takes a card from the deck lying on the table and turns it over: it's the Six of Wands.

"The tarot says no, that route is closed."

I'm disappointed. But, says Julián, I can read your cards: your cards about Elena Garro. Look, tell me what questions you have about her while you're shuffling the cards, tell me and then pass the deck to me.

There are so many questions that I can't immediately think of even one. Then they come:

First: Was she ever really in love with Paz?

Second: Was she, despite it all, in fact a friend of Fernando Gutiérrez Barrios, or was she just pretending to be his friend to gain favor and avoid being killed?

Third: To what extent was she paranoid and to what extent actually persecuted?

Fourth: Why didn't she go to Argentina with Bioy Casares?

The first card to come out is protection: the Nine of Swords. "Stress!" says Julián. "This card is for you." On the card you can see three triangles of swords and a king on his throne pierced by another sword. "The card," says Julián, "speaks to me of your doubts, the questions you have, but they are good, useful questions."

The threat card is the Ten of Wands and it's reversed. Under the sheath of ten wands, you can see a dragon biting its tail. "It's a complete circle," says Julián, "but in reverse. This is for you too; you're close to finishing your research, but you need to look at it in reverse to understand it; you have to turn it around."

For an instant I think of that matter of reverses, how Elena liked the reverse side of things, then we are on to the questions. Was she ever in love with Paz? The card is the Two of Cups. The image is of two goblets and, below, the figure of Cupid with bow drawn and arrow at the ready. "Yes," says Julián, "she was in love. This is the classic card of love and the two cups are related to marriage. There's no doubt at all that she was in love with him."

In terms of her relationship with the shady politician and head of secret police, Gutiérrez Barrios, the card is the Two of Pentacles, in reverse. It's the card for perfection, says Julián, but perfection isn't always a good thing. "It's an ambiguous card; the answer isn't clear." In the second round for that question is the Eight of Cups, which has an eclipse below. "That means more ambiguity. Although it does seem there was some level of real appreciation there," Julián tells me.

How much was paranoia and how much was she persecuted? First is the Knight of Cups and then the Page of Pentacles. The images are: a young boy with his eyes blindfolded, above a crab on the moon; a naked young man with a scythe, holding a gold coin, on top of a grasshopper. "Pages tend to take a leading role," says Julián, "and that gentleman is rather childish. Setting aside whether or not her fear was real, it had to do with her narcissism."

Why didn't she go away with Bioy Casares? The Seven of Cups. On the card is a rather sullen-looking baby being born from an egg, under the stars. My face immediately shows surprise. "Elena aborted a child by Bioy," I tell Julián. "That's it," he says, "that must be the reason. You found the answer yourself."

LAST NIGHT I DREAMED OF YOU, ELENA GARRO

In this underground room with its high, glass ceilings, wearing a yellow dress, sitting at the table where I write to you today. You were looking through your own archive, urgently scrutinizing, examining, consulting the papers. That was the whole dream: you, searching your own documents for answers about yourself.

FUR COATS

Money was always a problem. Getting it and keeping it. In the archives of the years when they didn't have two cents to rub together, there are receipts for hundreds of dollars for fur coats from Bloomingdale's. The money Paz sent slipped through their fingers like water. Helena Paz was particularly extravagant. In an unpublished story, Elena tells of how her daughter once squandered the whole monthly check on a lilac dress. The poem "Insomnia" says:

Elena Garro Papers.

Looking for money!
A difficult quest.
It's so well hidden.
Easier to find the face of God.

Cristales de tiempo, p. 227.

DIVINE PROVIDENCE

In 1980, her luck began to improve (at least in certain aspects, as will be seen). Emilio Carballido, whom Elena called "Divine Providence," visited them in Madrid that year and Elena gave him the manuscripts of *Andamos huyendo, Lola*, *Testimonios sobre Mariana*, *Reencuentro de personajes*, and *La casa junto al río*. The books that she'd written over almost fifteen years, but never published, began to reach readers. Emilio Carballido became her literary agent and *Testimonios sobre Mariana*, which would win the Juan Grijalbo novel prize, was published in 1981. In 1983, her play *El árbol* was awarded the Muestra Nacional theater prize in the best "author" (in the masculine) category. That year the Elenas also moved to an apartment in Paris at Ave. Duquesne 40, and then to another on Champ de Mars, lent to them by the family of ex-president Giscard d'Estaing. According to Vilma Fuentes, they stopped liking the apartment when one of their cats fell from the third floor and they moved again to the 16th arrondissement.

Testimonios sobre Elena Garro, p. 450.

Elena Garro, la pérdida del reino, p. 72.

In 1990, Octavio Paz was awarded the Nobel Prize

in Literature. Around that time, Helena Paz patched things up with her father and found a job at the Mexican embassy in Paris, although her poor physical and mental health meant she was periodically absent from work. She started to suffer severe emotional crises, was taking barbiturates, drinking heavily, and becoming increasingly dysfunctional. On one occasion, after being run over, she had a nervous breakdown and had to be committed. Octavio Paz covered the medical costs.

Elena Garro Papers.

In Elena's diaries from those years, there are long lists of Spanish-French vocabulary and other notes related to her study of French. There are poems, lists of books, sums, a zodiac wheel, and whole pages with her daughter's name, written in a timid, trembling hand.

THE MADWOMAN IN THE ATTIC

When I tell a science fiction author that I'm writing about Elena Garro, she says, "She was mad." A literature PhD student comments, "She was a raving loony." A children's book editor offers the opinion that "she flipped her lid." A compulsive reader asks, "Wasn't she a spy who went crazy?" A male friend asks why I find it so difficult to capture Elena Garro and, because I'm tired and don't feel like talking, I hear myself say, "It's 'cause she was mad."

There's absolutely no doubt that Elena wasn't a great example of mental health. This was particularly true toward the second half of her life, although it can be asked how much of that was nature and how much nurture. The problem with the word "madwoman" is that for centuries it's been an umbrella term for any female suffering depression, any woman who is an activist, is frightened, angry, extroverted, or rebellious. A way of dismissing them all without taking into account the complexity of their emotions, their situations, and the role society has had in shaping their circumstances. There's a reason why psychiatric hospitals of the last century were largely full of women.

Elena Garro, la pérdida del reino, p. 73.

Vilma Fuentes says that Elena "confused reality and fiction, but without being mad. When I say mad as a March hare, I'm not talking about people in a lunatic asylum; it's something else."

In *La cuarta casa*, which was filmed by José Antonio Cordero during the last four years of Elena's life, she seems perfectly lucid and coherent. She's also angry. In one of her notebooks there is a handwritten quotation by Lord Byron: "My solitude is solitude no more, / But peopled with the furies." Fury, an emotion frowned upon for the women of her time and still frowned upon in ours, is a recurrent theme in her work and is at the root of her activism and her personality. In 1947, she wrote this poem about her anger. The title is "A mi susituta en el tiempo" (To My [Female] Substitute in Time).

Elena Garro Papers.

Cristales de tiempo, p. 123.

When in the sea, only the lost pounding
of waves
and no trace of this teardrop is left
in memory
you, my friend who still waits for me
beyond this time,
will find my anger,
my rage at the mess they have made
of this world.

The following exchange between Bárbara and her daughter (also named Bárbara) takes place in her novel *Primer amor*:

"Are you sad, Mom?" asked Bárbara, looking at her mother.

"Me, sad?... I'm angry."

Novelas breves (Novellas), p. 404.

A POEM TO ELENA GARRO

Last night I saw you, Elena Garro.
I went to the pharmacy at half past midnight
to buy medicine for my son.
I saw you farther down the aisle in the white light,
draped in your panther furs.

You seemed disorientated.
Looked perplexedly at a menstrual cup,
and put a jar of anti-aging cream in your purse.

I saw you making friends with the cashier
and stroking the night watchman's dog.
I saw your look of disgust when a man
with dreads and a hat approached.

Maybe he reminded you of those hairy young men
in Dary's Café in New York.
It would have made you feel old, alone
and, as always,
out of
place.

We went out into the night, followed by
the shadow of one of your black cats.

Are you hungry, Elena? Are you cold?
What do you think of this poem?
Of me speaking to your ghost at midnight
and toying with the *I Ching* and tarot cards.

You know the answer, so tell me
just how much alienation can be tolerated,
what dose of eccentricity
borne.

I don't know why I'm asking you
because I know you're leaving.

Your frail, thin
body
moves away,
amorphous specter
of cigarette
smoke.

RANCOR AND REPENTANCE

The hatred Elena felt for Paz is summed up in these words she spoke to Gabriela Mora:

Lectura múltiple, p. 33.

> You see, Gabriela, you only get one enemy in this life, and that's enough. And my enemy is Paz...I want you to know once and for all...that I live in spite of him...I studied in spite of him, I spoke in spite of him, I had lovers in spite of him, I wrote in spite of him, and I defended the Indians in spite of him, I wrote about politics in spite of him; in short, absolutely everything that I am is in spite of him. That's why he persecutes my family and friends.

But one of her last known texts, dating from 1989, is a letter to Octavio Paz, in which she asks forgiveness:

"Una carta postrera de Elena Garro a Octavio Paz" (A final letter from Elena Garro to Octavio Paz).

> I've been meaning to write to you for some time to ask your forgiveness for all the disasters, misfortunes, and suffering I've caused you. Believe me, I'm asking your pardon after a long, long

> period of introspection, of examining my conscience, and analyzing my execrable behavior. Sorry, I can't stop crying. Yes, I'm crying my heart out. How could I have been so stupid? So frivolous? So thoughtless? All these years later, I don't understand why. And you used to say I was so intelligent! And out of vanity, I took you seriously! It tortures me. I can see that everything you said to me (except for the part about my intelligence) was true.

It isn't easy to be sure if she's serious in this because she was in the habit of feigning repentance or courtesy when she wanted something. And what she wanted from Paz on that occasion was for her nephew Jesús to be relieved of his post in the consulate and for someone to take care of her cats when she died.

In an interview, Patricia Vega asked if she repented any of her actions, and she replied, "I haven't repented anything because I know I'd do it all again, and the more I repent it, the more I do it. But I'm thinking of making an act of contrition, a serious one to a priest, before I die." Her daughter said that Elena "never admitted to her mistakes." And that "she always used to say she had no regrets." But then in another interview, when asked what she repented, she said, "a lot of things. I was always putting my foot in it." And she told Antonio Cordero that she did regret so much foolishness, said that she'd been a very silly child, and later very shallow, and if she could, she'd blot out her whole life.

Díalogos con Elena Garro, p. 1110.

Memorias, p. 361.

Lectura múltiple, p. 200.

La cuarta casa.

RUSSIA, RUSSIA, RUSSIA

During the final decades of her life, Elena became obsessed with Russia. It's said that she believed she was a descendent of the tsars and she wanted to write a novel in which Greta Garbo was really a Russian princess. As research for the novel, she was constantly reading Russian history and Russian authors, filling whole notebooks with jottings and quotations. She told Vilma Fuentes that "the history [of Russia] is so abracadabrant" and went on, "I've made so many notes, Vilma, I feel dizzy just looking at them. But I want to finish it before I die. It's a book that looks at both sides; the side of what was destroyed and the side that took power."

Lectura múltiple, p. 217.

I read her notes about Russia, all of them, all of those quotations and interminable lists of books, books, books, and I see myself as she was, obsessed, chasing ghosts, trying to understand the abracadabrant story of Elena Garro.

THE VOICE OF THE SUN

The Casa Alvarado is an eighteenth-century building in the Andalusian and Moorish styles, now painted orange with white trim. It was in this house in Coyoacán that Octavio Paz died, a few months after the library in his home was destroyed by fire—it's said that Elena had announced her desire for it to be burned not long before that accident. And it was here, of all places, that I've come in search of the voice of Elena Garro.

Elena Garro: los recuerdos sin porvenir, p. 111.

I walk through the gardens, between ferns and yellow columns, and then enter the sound archive. Today, the Casa Alvarado is the home of the Fonoteca Nacional. I sit in front of a screen and search the archives for the voice of Elena Garro. There are several dramatic readings of her short stories, lectures by critics and academics about her works, and a few radio programs dedicated to her. But I can find only one interview, for Radio Educación, recorded in 1996. The topic of the program is the city of Puebla, where Elena was born.

"I love Puebla. I have good memories of it," says her threadlike voice. "The first is of a garden with thermal pools that I went to with my mother and cousins. I fell over there and got a bad cut on my head."

Despite having spent very little time in the city, she is interviewed as a native *Poblana*, and she assumes that role with pride: "I'm thrilled. Yes, so proud. I really like the idea that we Poblanos are different from everyone else." It's a high-pitched, fragile voice, interrupted every so often by a deep, dry cough. Elena used to say that she hadn't taken up acting due to her weak voice, because she got fed up with always being asked to speak louder.

People who heard her speak before she developed emphysema also remember a low-pitched voice. They describe the contrast between its tone and her merciless ingenuity: "Elena's words in conversation—spoken very quietly, in a sweet, soft tone that seemed to emerge from the mouth of an angel, in that provincial accent that she never lost—were spoken rapidly and contained hedonistic cruelty."

Vilma Fuentes in *Lectura múltiple*, p. 216.

An artist of conversation, of discourse. Her work retains that oral quality and is a rich source of Mexicanisms, adages, and commonplace expressions. At her best, witnesses describe Elena Garro as a heavenly body: a luminous, golden center of gravity. "She had what is often called *duende*, magical charm, something angelic that goes far beyond the American idea of sex appeal. Her attraction was solar," said Elena Poniatowska. Those who knew her speak of a beauty that was so much more than mere appearance; China Mendoza said, "it was total beauty, not for its perfection but its distinction, for being so sure of itself." And they say

Poniatowska, *Obras reunidas*, p. 89.

"Memoranda," in Garro, *Obras reunidas III*, p. xii.

that it was her voice, her words, that robed her physical beauty in something superior. Emanuel Carballo said that "when she was silent, she was good-looking, but hearing her made her dazzlingly beautiful."

Elena Garro, la pérdida del reino, p. 29.

I'd hoped to hear her sing in one of those recordings. Helena said that her mother sang very well; she specialized in corridos and was compared to Lucha Reyes. I'd also hoped to hear her laugh, because what I like most in the Elena I've read about is her sense of humor, her ironic, joyful, or caustic laughter. In "La memoria" (Memory)—an unpublished story in the Princeton archive—Elena recalls (rightly or wrongly) that her characteristic laugh came from her grandmother, Francisca, and she finds the origin of her existence in that laugh: "Grandmother Francisca burst out laughing and that was the first time I heard laughter. I believe that I began to be in the world after hearing that laughter."

Memorias, p. 324.

Elena Garro Papers.

THE *TIME OF ENTHUSIASM*

My mother lent me a 1976 Chilean edition of the *I Ching*. She's used it so frequently that it's falling apart now, and no longer has a front cover or spine. My mother puts a great deal of faith in it because, on the day of the 1985 earthquake she got the hexagram for "shock." "Everything falls down," the *I Ching* told my mother. (On the date of that earthquake, Elena was in Paris, certain that Octavio Paz had died. During the 1957 quake, she was at the house of the poet Guadalupe Amor, and Poniatowska says that Elena was in such a state that she threatened to throw herself from the balcony.)

Poniatowska, *Obras reunidas*, p. 86.

I once cast an *I Ching* with my mother and now I'm going through the instructions to remind myself what to do: toss the three coins six times, note from bottom up if the result corresponds to one or two horizontal bars, look in the table for the number of the resulting hexagram and then read.

My question for the *I Ching* is as follows: If Elena Garro had been born in 1988, if she was now, like me, thirty-four years old, would she have been happier than she was in her own time?

Vilma Fuentes says that Elena Garro would have liked to have been born in a past era. "But even as a ghost, it's no easy task to appear in an epoch that has disappeared." I, on the other hand, think that Elena would have been happier in the future, and the *I Ching* agrees with me. It responds with Number 16: Enthusiasm. It seems very optimistic about the possibility of a millennial Elena Garro: "The celestial bodies do not deviate from their orbits," it tells me. Enthusiasm "can unify mass movements." It states emphatically, "Thunder comes resounding out of the earth." "The time of ENTHUSIASM," it says, "derives from the fact that there is at hand an eminent man who is in sympathy with the spirit of the people and acts in accord with it." The *I Ching* of 1976 says "man," but it clearly means to say "woman."

Díalogos con Elena Garro, p. 1380.

THE HOMELAND AND ALL THAT STUFF

In 1991, the Elenas returned to Mexico for the first time in almost twenty years at the invitation of José María Fernández Unsaín, who was at the head of the General Society of Writers of Mexico (SOGEM). Elena told Vilma Fuentes that she almost changed her mind at the last moment.

Testimonios sobre Elena Garro, p. 466.

> That evening, while we were having dinner—continued Elena—I said to Rosario Casco...who had been sent for me: "I'm not going," but she called her boss...José María Unsaín. I told him, "I'm not going. I'm not going." He got so angry it frightened me. "Okay, I'll go," and I went. I didn't want to, Vilma, I knew it would be a catastrophe, but everyone, including Helenita, said that I was crazy, that I should go, return to my country, that I needed to go and see things for myself, the Homeland and all that stuff.

She also told Vilma Fuentes that she was overcome by emotion when she arrived: "I was in floods of tears as I got off the plane...I was in Mexico again. It was stronger than me." And the first person to visit was her friend Rodolfo Echeverría, brother to the former president of Mexico. Ibid.

She traveled to Guadalajara and then to Aguascalientes, where her play *El árbol* was being performed. From there she went to Monterrey and said about that city, "You feel like you've come back home there. They fêted me. It was where I received the most tributes." "The only place where I've seen women having power in their own right, without the need for manipulation. They are like guardians of the arts, like patrons in olden times." After that she traveled to Mexico City, where she had an "awful shock": "as if the Devil had passed and blown out the candles." "It all seemed very strange to me, I didn't recognize anything except the chicken tacos with guacamole, which I ate every day." She also went to Cuernavaca to visit her sister Deva, and later to Puebla, where she was given the keys to the city and the *Cédula real*, a certificate of royal approval granted to distinguished Poblanos. She didn't make it to Oxolotán, Tabasco State, where the members of the Laboratorio de Teatro Campesino e Indígena—a communitarian, mass, indigenous, and rural theater project—named the first generation of the group "Elena Garro" and staged six of her works. She returned to Cuernavaca and from there went to Mexico City for a tribute in the Bellas Artes with Emilio Carballido, Héctor Azar, Margo Glantz, Silvia Molina, Carmen Boullosa, and Guillermo Samperio.

Ibid., p. 468.

Ibid., p. 470.

Elena finally returned to Paris, deep in debt

because they were living on the salary of her daughter, who had asked for an unpaid leave of absence to accompany her, and because before leaving they had outfitted themselves with coats and dresses for the trip.
Ibid., p. 474.
On March 10, 1992, she writes in her diary about how cold it felt everywhere.

MASKS

If Elena Garro was anything, she was a true character. It's no surprise that she was the inspiration for so many literary works. She appears in "Las dos Elenas" (The Two Elenas), a short story by Carlos Fuentes; "La continuación" (The Continuation) by Silvina Ocampo; *La pérdida del reino* by José Bianco; *El sueño de los héroes* (The Dream of Heroes) by Adolfo Bioy Casares; *Sunstone* by Octavio Paz; and *Flores negras* (Black Flowers) by Vilma Fuentes, among many others.

She said that it didn't upset her when she was portrayed as a repulsive character:

> The act of writing is an act of personal freedom. I've never complained about being used as a character in poems, novels, and short stories. I remember that Carlitos Fuentes wrote a story called "Las dos Elenas." The whole of Mexico was saying that it was Chata and me. There were people trying to set me against the author. That seemed ridiculous. It's fine for anybody to fabricate fictional characters from real people.

Protagonistas, p. 495.

She also said that she wasn't annoyed when Paz wrote about her in *Sunstone*:

Ibid., p. 495.

> We read and reread it together. "You're not offended, are you?" asked Paz. "No, you have a right to say what you think," I told him. And what he thought was to call me "an old animal hide, a bag of bones," or something like that…A poet mythologizes and Paz wanted to exorcise me by turning me into a devil. All poets have done it. That's what poetic creation is for.

Nevertheless, she sometimes seemed to be more affected by that mixing of reality and fiction; for example, when José Bianco sent her *La pérdida del reino*, based on the period when they were both living in Paris, Elena wrote to him:

José Bianco Papers.

> Tell me, was that how life was, or was it the way you saw it? It's an idiotic question. Novels are never life. They are novels. I couldn't critique your book. Can you see a fly when it gets in your own eye? That Laura says a lot of foolishness. Thank goodness she disappears at the age of twenty-seven! Then, catastrophe! Any intelligent person reading her would say, "That woman isn't going to have a happy ending." What a pity your novel isn't like life, which comes to an end. Reading it has made me even more certain about a feeling that had

> been haunting me: "How long are we going to survive ourselves?"

Elena asked him if life was like that or if that was how he saw it, and that question contains the need to search for answers to experience, or at least to the perception of experience, in literature. The affirmation with which she responds to her own question indicates the impossibility of finding answers.

Elena often had to clarify that her novels were not biographical. Or were, but not completely, not always, only to some extent. She was irritated by simplistic, autobiographical readings. For instance, she once said, "There's a determined effort to confuse my literature with my private life, particularly my married life. I'm fed up with it! Absolutely everything is O.P. It's a total pain in the ass." In relation to her novel *Testimonios sobre Mariana*, she said:

Ibid.

> If you think there are real-life people in *Mariana*, you're wrong. Although it's true, I did use aspects of certain living or dead people to create a single character. Remember Ortega y Gasset: "what is not lived experience is academia." And think of Dostoyevsky and Balzac too, "the novel is life." That doesn't mean that what I write in *Mariana* is simply a tracing of my life on paper. I think all novels are romans à clef or they aren't novels.

Protagonistas, p. 494.

On the other hand, in relation to the same book, she writes in a letter, "I warn you that every phrase,

Lectura múltiple, p. 331.

every character, every situation is authentic. What I find difficult is to order, to ELIMINATE situations because when I put everything in, it doesn't sound true to life." It is in this negotiation between the lifelike and unlifelike, the authentic and the artificial, memory and fantasy, fidelity and betrayal, that, in general, a great part of literature exists, and this is particularly true of Elena's work. Her own life was the creation of one and several characters: masks worn for others and sometimes for herself.

SMILE FOR THE CAMERA

A friend who knew Elena Garro told me the following anecdote—that she, in turn, had heard from someone else:

One day when Elena was living with Paz in Paris, there was a reception at the Guatemalan embassy. Paz told Elena to get dressed to accompany him. She replied that she didn't want to go.

"I'm not going."

"Yes, you are."

"No, I'm not."

"Yes, you are."

Elena finally got dressed, as always very elegantly, and didn't say another word all the way to the embassy. When they arrived, she opened her mouth again: she'd painted all her teeth black.

NO NOTHING

Elena returned to Mexico in 1993. It was to be her last long journey. She packed her books into sixty boxes and took her thirteen cats with her. In Cuernavaca, she moved into Calle Manantiales 3, in the Chapultepec neighborhood, in an apartment that had belonged to her sister Estrella. And she continued to cause controversy, like when she said that Unsaín—who, through SOGEM, was helping her to claim her royalties—had tried to cheat her (it seems clear that this was not the case, and that the confusion was due to a letter they needed for the royalties to be paid).

Lectura múltiple, p. 159.

In José Antonio Cordero's documentary, Elena speaks of this last stage of her life:

La cuarta casa.

> And what was it you expected here in Mexico?
> Nothing, I didn't want to come back.
>
> But what were you promised?
> I didn't expect anything from what I was promised. I know it's easy to make promises and difficult to keep them.

But what were you promised?
Oh...A house.

I haven't written anything since I arrived in Cuernavaca.
Why not?
I don't know. Cuernavaca depresses me so much. This small apartment and the heat.

What was the last thing you wrote?
An article about my arrival in Mexico.

Elena, are you happy?
No.
Why not?
Who knows. But I'm not unhappy either. I'm neutral.

What does happiness mean for you?
Something that can't be achieved in this world, if it can be achieved at all.

And why can't it be achieved?
Because we're evil.

And we got here and there was no house, no job, no nothing.

THE QUEEN OF SWORDS—REVERSED

Your books and your life are populated by ghosts. Dark, disturbing, persecutory presences, some of flesh and blood and others you invented, but that for you were no less real. Now you too are a ghost, with whom some of us speak. I read Luna Miguel speaking to you in a book called *El coloquio de las perras* (The She-dogs Speak Out). She says:

El coloquio de las perras, p. 14.

> Dear Elena, there's a reason they called you the outcast queen. Or in the words of María Luisa Mendoza, "the poorest queen." I've learned that you are that queen for reasons that have nothing to do with your work. Nobody has yet allowed you to be crowned as "the best [female] writer in Mexico."

Emmanuel Carballo called you "Her Majesty, Elena I" and for me you are the Queen of Swords, that queen who appeared in a tarot reading done for your friend Enrique, who said it was you. You truly were a force to be reckoned with although you called yourself a pacifist. You liked St. Michael because he protects the world with his sword. You went through life with your sword unsheathed, your tongue a sharp dagger that spared no one. And although you lived through many horrendous situations without complaint, you also knew how to rebel, to criticize, to demand, to fight, even to be rash, cruel, bitchy, arrogant, and treacherous. At times it seems that you thought yourself invincible, like a Queen of Swords; at others the first head you wanted to chop off was your own. It's said that this tarot queen represents discernment, rationality, total control of the emotions—not exactly your strong points—but in Enrique's reading, the card came out reversed, and that is exactly what I think you might have been: the Queen of Swords Reversed.

Whichever way you look at it, for me you are the Queen of Swords and that will be the title of this book, to please you, someone who preferred monarchy, someone who—don't pretend otherwise—would have loved to be a queen. Who wanted to be a queen but ended up a witch. A witch queen—of course they exist—hounded and delirious, living apart from the world with your cats, reading tarot spreads and the constellations. I say all this to you with love.

EIGHTY-SIX DWELLINGS

Garro Velásquez and Schmid-huber de la Mora, "Elena Garro, dramaturga" in *Teatro completo,* p. xxxv.

Her nephew, Jesús Garro, calculated a total of eighty-six dwelling places for Elena Garro: "including houses, apartments, hotels, convents, a refuge for Catholic women in Spain, and, finally, one that she longed for all her life: a solid home in the Panteón de la Paz in Cuernavaca."

Memorias, p. 394.

Helena wrote that when her mother told her about her childhood in Iguala, her brothers and sisters, their pranks, she always ended by saying, "I was so happy at home." Elena never called the house where she lived with her daughter and Paz her home.

Elena Garro Papers.

In a letter from 1986, she writes to Emilio Carballido: "I dream of wooden houses, pretty, three-story houses with large, clean, bright rooms and Helena and I playing hide and seek, unable to stop laughing, while the visitors make small talk in the living room."

ON TIME AND MEMORY

Elena said that when she was a child, she and her sister Deva used to slide down the banister, and one time she fell off, hit her head, and remembers nothing of the following three months. About that period of amnesia, she wrote:

> Real murder is wiping from one's own and other people's memories the image of someone, that someone not only ceases to exist, but never existed, isn't even a shadow. That three-month interruption of memory is a mystery as important as my first memory.

Elena Garro Papers.

Existence, says Elena, is remembering.

Her whole body of work can be read as a treatise on time and memory. She said she'd learned her conception of time from her father—who knew about Buddhism, read Eisenstein—and from the Nahuas in Iguala. Not a linear time, but cyclical or simultaneous, depending on the space and the mood, where present, past, future, and other unnamable times coexist. And a memory that makes time, that is time and existence. In her work, there are houses in which time doesn't elapse, days of the week that are people, where there are invisible clocks, ghosts condemned to repeating their actions, and parallel historical times.

Teatro completo, p. 35.

> Have you thought, Don Fernando of the Seven and Five, about where Mondays have gone? We haven't heard anything of them for seven days.

Ibid., p. 41.

> We are Monday, fallen stars in the night of Sunday.

Ibid., p. 144.

> I hear you, sir, and I say that time lasts and doesn't. It can be as long as a day's illness or short, as short as my grandmother's ninety years, which were portrayed in the blink of my grandfather's eyes.

Ibid., p. 227.

> Time, time, always time… Maybe, Colonel, our time has run out and a new, unpredictable time is beginning. Maybe time is finite…

Andamos huyendo, Lola, p. 259.

> Nothing is harder than "making time." How do you make ""time""? Perhaps by walking backwards.

Recollections, p. 5.

> On this street there is a large stone house with a square porch and a garden filled with plants and dust. Time does not pass there: the air stood still after so many tears were shed.

...memory contains all times and their order is unpredictable...

Ibid., p. 6.

Without the ticking, the room and its occupants entered a new and melancholy time where gestures and voices moved in the past. Doña Ana, her husband, the children, and Félix were changed into memories of themselves without a future, lost in a yellow, individual light that separated them from reality to make them only personages of memory.

Ibid., p. 14.

Life is made up of absurd pieces of time and odd objects.

Testimonios sobre Mariana, p. 7.

OBITUARIES

José Bianco died in Buenos Aires in 1986.

Poniatowska, *Obras reunidas*, p. 84.

Octavio Paz died on April 19, 1998. On his death, Elena said, "He's gone before me. He'll be up there above to receive me. I forgive him, I know he's forgiven me, and I hope to join him soon. Death is living forever."

Elena Garro, la pérdida del reino, p. 79.

Four months later, on August 22, 1998, Elena Garro died. A handful of people said their farewells at her funeral in Cuernavaca.

On March 8, 1999, Adolfo Bioy Casares died. I visited his grave in the Recoleta cemetery in Buenos Aires. I couldn't find it alone because it has no name and was guided by a gravedigger, who told me that the plaque had fallen off and been thrown into the bottom of the crypt because the Bioy heirs wouldn't pay the upkeep. (Silvina Ocampo is in the same cemetery but there is no name on her grave either.)

On March 30, 2014, at the age of seventy-four, Helena Paz Garro died, one day before the centenary of her father's birth and the official celebrations organized for the occasion.

QUESTIONS ABOUT DEATH

What did Elena Garro believe about death?

In an interview, she told Reynol Pérez Vázquez that she thought it was passing "from one state to another." "It can't be the end of this life. So many things, and for it all to finish. Dying is passing from this place to another dimension, call it heaven, call it purgatory, call it hell," she told him.

Lectura múltiple, p. 203.

Her play *Un hogar sólido* is a dialogue between the dead in a family crypt as they await Judgement Day. Those souls imagine that when the Apocalypse arrives, they will be changed into "all things." And after "having learned to be all things, the Lance of Michael, center of the universe, will appear and in its light the divine host of angels, and we will enter the celestial order."

Teatro completo, p. 12.

Clara, the protagonist of the play *La señora en su balcón*, thinks that on her death she will go to Nineveh, the lost capital of the Neo-Assyrian Empire, to encounter infinite time. She imagines death as her last escape, the flight from herself, the only necessary flight, a great leap to "enter the silvered city" that is "trembling in time like a perfect, translucent drop of water waiting for me, untouched by tempos and useless words."

Ibid., p. 93.

In *Recollections of Things to Come*, Martín Moncada says that he is certain that death is a "perfect state," the moment when humans fully recover their "other memory." Death as recollection. Doña Matilde, on the other hand, is afraid that dying would be wanting to wake and never, ever waking again.

Recollections, p. 29 and 211.

How did she imagine her own death?

She once conceived of it this way:

> I want to die in my sleep, and for my burial, I sometimes imagine a bell tower, and that I'm very happy there, listening to the bells and watching the people entering the church to pray for me. I want to be an angel, although I think I was a demon.

Poniatowska, *Obras reunidas,* p. 85.

José Antonio Alarcón López told Patricia Rosas Lopátegui that, a year before she passed on, sometime around the Day of the Dead, he was with Elena in her home in Cuernavaca. After having Marián cookies and milk, Elena told him that she wanted to die. He said not to think of such things, but she insisted. She remembered a song that she used to love, a "very Mexican" song—the northern *Cruz de Madera*. And she sang it:

Cristales de tiempo, p. 253.

A very ordinary wooden cross,
is what I ask for when I die.
I don't want luxuries or adobe tables.
I don't want a casket costing millions.
All I want is for songs to be sung,
so the death of a poor man is a grand fiesta.

She said that she'd like to have a great many pink flowers on her death.

UNDER THE BOUGAINVILLEA

The gravestone says:

The Solid
Home of:
Elena Garro Navarro
Dec.-11-1916-August-22-1998
Helena Laura Paz Garro
Dec.-12-1939-March-30-2014
I am only memory
and the memory that one has of me.
And as memory contains all times
and their order is unpredictable...
Memory returns those days to me intact.
Jesús Garro (Shorty) and family.

There's an article published in 2014 in which the journalist María Teresa Priego Broca recounts a visit to Elena Garro's grave in the Jardines de la Paz cemetery in Cuernavaca. That year, she found an unmarked gravestone. But since then the Garro family have had a small mausoleum, what is known as a *casita*, built for Elena and her daughter. The casita is white, with a thatch roof, on which rests a small chimney and the statuette of a yellow, smiling cat. Below the roof, the epitaph is written in black. Inside the casita is a small space with a photo of Elena embracing her daughter, an old stone cross, a red votive candle, a plaster or plastic painted figurine of the Archangel Michael, another photo of Elena, with her arms around a man (possibly her nephew), a wooden cross embossed with silver, a number of ceramic figurines of cats, and a casket, embossed in aluminum with the word Choupet—I imagine it must contain the ashes of one of her cats. On the lower part of the metal door is a reproduction of Remedios Varo's *El paraíso de los gatos* (Cats' Paradise). The cats in the painting live in a green landscape, with a lake and plenty of space to run around, climb trees, and hunt birds. There is also a tower for looking out the window and sheltering from the rain, and a mobile so the cats can chase the threads, paintbrushes, and ribbons fluttering in the wind. Apparently, Elena didn't like Remedios Varo, said she was another of Paz's "crazy" admirers, and treated her badly.

Elena Garro: los recuerdos sin porvenir, p. 83.

The tomb is adorned with red and purple bougainvillea and a large ficus, which offers shade.

FAREWELL REVERSED

How to finish this book? Not with your death, because the story doesn't end there. Because your life touched lives that still continue, stories that go on, because your work itself has had a history, a story, since your death. An unjust story and, at least so far, largely silenced. But after so many years of being a cult author, your books are now being reissued and reaching more and more eyes, which are giving them new life.

There are many mysteries still to be cleared up. Many lost or hidden letters and secrets buried with the dead. And some other answers that I'm sure even the dead don't have.

I've spent two years, six months, and two days inside your head, your life, Elena Garro, and it's an exhausting place to be. I reread your story over and over, the different versions—they really are very different: the saint, the madwoman, the heroine, the comedian—and you continue to be eternally trapped in them. And as though I don't already know the ending, on each reading I find myself hoping that this time you'll manage to save yourself. But no. Each time, your charm, your likeability, your intelligence, and your brilliance become victims of history, of others, and (above all, perhaps) yourself. Whenever I return to your origins, I wish you a happy ending and I don't know how to write it, except in reverse: starting your life in death and ending it in childhood. And now that I remember, that's what I'm going to do, because you always liked reverses, because you say that everything happened to you in reverse.

So, we'll finish with this image, Elena: with you in Iguala, running in the garden, climbing a plum tree, slingshot in hand, looking up at the fiery sky with the sun setting behind the hills.

SOURCES, SPRINGS, AND PUDDLES

The majority of the quotations in this book come from the titles listed below. Others are from letters and documents in the archives of Elena Garro and José Bianco in the Firestone Library, Princeton University.

Bianco, José, *La pérdida del reino*. Adriana Hidalgo, 2004.

Bioy Casares, Adolfo, *El sueño de los héroes*. Emecé, 1984.

Bioy Casares, Adolfo, *Memorias*. Alfaguara, 2022.

Cabrera, Rafael, *Debo olvidar que existí. Retrato inédito de Elena Garro*. Debate, 2017.

Carballo, Emmanuel, *Protagonistas de la literatura mexicana*. Porrúa, 2003.

Cordero, José Antonio, *La cuarta casa, un retrato de Elena Garro*. Consejo Nacional para la Cultura y las Artes (CONACULTA), el Centro de Capacitación Cinematográfica (CCC) y el Instituto Mexicano de Cinematografía (IMCINE), 2002.

Domínguez Michael, Christopher, *Octavio Paz en su siglo*. Debolsillo, 2019.

Enriquez, Mariana, *La hermana menor, un retrato de Silvina Ocampo*. Universidad Diego Portales, 2014.

Garro, Elena, *Andamos huyendo, Lola*. Mortiz, 1980.

Garro, Elena, *Antología de Geney Beltrán Félix*. Cal y arena, 2016.

Garro, Elena, *Cristales de tiempo*, edited, preliminary study, and notes by Patricia Rosas Lopátegui. La Moderna and Rosas Lopátegui Publishing, 2018.

Garro, Elena, *Cuentos completos*, prologue by Geney Beltrán Félix. Alfaguara, 2017.

Garro, Elena, *Diálogos con Elena Garro Vol. 1. Antes y después del 68*, edited, preliminary study, and notes by Patricia Rosas Lopátegui. Gedisa, 2020.

Garro, Elena, *Diálogos con Elena Garro Vol. 2. El retorno del exilio*, edited, preliminary study, and notes by Patricia Rosas Lopátegui. Gedisa, 2020.

Garro, Elena, *Inés*. Grijalbo, 1995.

Garro, Elena, *Material de lectura,* introductory notes by Cristina Rivera Garza and Marco Aurelio Carballo. UNAM, 2021.

Garro, Elena, *Memorias de España 1937*, prologue by Patricia Rosas Lopátegui. Salto de Página, 2013.

Garro, Elena, *Novelas breves*, prologue by Jazmina Barrera, edited by Álvaro Álvarez Delgado. Alfaguara, 2022.

Garro, Elena, *Novelas escogidas* (1981-1998), compilation and prologue by Geney Beltrán Félix. FCE, 2016.

Garro, Elena, *Obras reunidas III, novela*, prologue by María Luisa Mendoza and trigger warnings by Patricia Rosas Lopátegui. FCE, 2010.

Garro, Elena, *Los recuerdos del porvenir.* Alfaguara, 2021.

Garro, Elena, *Recollections of Things to Come*, translated with an introduction by Ruth L.C. Simms and drawings by Alberto Beltrán. University of Texas Press, 1969.

Garro, Elena, *Relatos recuperados*, prologue by Olivia Teroba. Benemérita Universidad Autónoma de Puebla and Ediciones del Lirio, 2023.

Garro, Elena, *Teatro completo,* prologue by Jesús Garro and Guillermo Schmidhuber. FCE, 2016.

Garro, Elena, *Testimonios sobre Mariana*. Grijalbo, 1981.

Garro, Elena, *The Week of Colors*, translated by Megan MacDowell. Two Lines Press, 2025.

Glantz, Margo, "Elena Garro: el color de la muerte," *Zama* 1, no. 1 (2008): 13-18. Also available from Alicante: Biblioteca virtual Miguel de Cervantes, 2021.

Glantz, Margo, "Elena Garro y sus enigmas," *Letras Femeninas* 29, no. 1, Número especial Vida y ficción en la obra de Elena Garro, edited by Lucía Melgar and Gabriela Mora (2003): 16-35.

Glantz, Margo, "Los enigmas de Elena Garro," *Anales de literatura hispanoamericana* 28 (1999): 681-697.

Guerriero, Leila (ed.), *Extremas*. Universidad Diego Portales, 2019.

Melgar, Lucía and Gabriela Mora (eds.), *Elena Garro: lectura múltiple de una personalidad compleja*. Benemérita Universidad Autónoma de Puebla, 2018.

Miguel, Luna, *El coloquio de las perras*. Capitán Swing Libros, 2019.

Paz, Octavio, *Early Poems 1935-1955*, various translators. New Directions, 1973.

Paz, Octavio, *Iconografía*, prologue, iconographic research, notes, and selection of texts by Rafael Vargas. FCE and Fondo Editorial Universidad Autónoma de Querétaro, 2020.

Paz, Octavio, *Obra poética* (1935-1988). Seix Barral, 1990.

Paz, Octavio, *Odi et amo: las cartas a Helena*, edited by Guillermo Sheridan. Siglo Veintiuno, 2021.

Paz Garro, Helena, *Memorias*. Debolsillo, 2019.

Pedroza, Liliana, *Andamos huyendo, Elena*. Tierra Adentro, 2007.

Poniatowska, Elena, *Obras reunidas*. FCE, 2012.

Puig, Carlos, "Espionaje a los intelectuales en los setentas: supuestas confidencias de Elena Garro sobre Oswald, en los archivos del caso Kennedy," *Proceso* 803 (1992).

Puig, Carlos, "La 'novia' mexicana de Lee Harvey Oswald y Gutiérrez Barrios." Milenio, November 2013.

Ramírez, Luis Enrique, *La ingobernable, encuentros y desencuentros con Elena Garro*. Raya en el agua, 2000.

Ramos, Laura, *Elena Garro: Los recuerdos sin porvenir*. Aguilar, 2023.

Ríos, Brenda, *Raras, ensayos sobre el amor, lo femenino, a voluntad creadora*. Turner, 2019.

Rosas Lopátegui, Patricia, *El asesinato de Elena Garro*, prologue by Elena Poniatowska. Universidad Autónoma del estado de Morelos and Porrúa, 2005.

Rosas Lopátegui, Patricia, *Testimonios sobre Elena Garro*. Ediciones Castillo, 2002.

Rosas Lopátegui, Patricia, *Yo solo soy memoria, biografía visual de Elena Garro*. Ediciones Castillo, 2000.

Rosas Lopátegui, Patricia, Rhina Toruño, and Elena Garro, "Elena Garro: Entrevista," *Hispamérica* 20, no. 60 (1991): 55–71.

Ruiz Parra, Emiliano, *Elena Garro, la pérdida del reino*. B*rigada para leer en libertad, 2023*.)

Sheridan, Guillermo, "La dama misteriosa, Elena Garro y el asesino de Kennedy." *Letras Libres*, May 7, 2017.

Sheridan, Guillermo, "Una carta postrera de Elena Garro a Octavio Paz." *Letras Libres*, September 13, 2017.

Toruño, Rita, *Encounter with Memory; Elena Garro Tells Her Life to Rhina Toruño*. Bloomington, IN: Palibrio, 2011.

THANKS

To María Fernanda Álvarez for her initiative and generosity. To the friends who read this book and contributed so much to it: César Tejeda, Isabel Zapata, Margarita García Robayo, Verónica Murguía, Emiliano Ruiz Parra, Luna Miguel, Pau Luque, Andrés Braithwaite, Diego Zúñiga, Marina Azahua, Francisco Carrillo, and Nayeli García. To Rafael Cabrera and Luigi Amara for lending me books impossible to buy. To Mariana Enriquez and Mercedes Halfon for your help in following up on leads in Argentina. To Jorge Comensal, Aurelia Cortés Peyron, Isabel Zapata, Marina Azahua and Elisa Díaz Castelo for playing the question game. To Julián Herbert for his tarot reading. To the Casa Estudio Cien Años de Soledad for their welcome during the writing of this book. To Fonca's Jóvenes Creadores program for the grant I was given during the same period. To Javier Guerrero and the whole archival team in the Firestone Library for their kind advice. To Cecilia García-Huidobro, Valentina Litvan, Nancy Calomarde, and Alejandro Lámbarry for sharing the archive fever. To Paula Canal and Andrea Montejo for their indispensable, unquestioning support. To John Wray and Joanna Delgado Chiaberto for their friendship and for welcoming me into their home while I was doing research. To Christina MacSweeney for the careful, brilliant, and loving translation of this book. To María Teresa Velázquez, María Elisa Velázquez, Adolphe Lechenberg, Érika Morales, and all those who have looked after my son while I was writing. To Alejandro Zambra, for his contributions to this book and for always being a solid home.

And to everyone who has kept the memory of Elena Garro alive.

JAZMINA BARRERA was born in Mexico City in 1988. She is the author of six books in Spanish: *Cuerpo extraño, Cuaderno de faros, Linea nigra, Los nombres de los animals* (a Children's Book), *Punto de cruz,* and *La reina de espadas*. She has also co-written the books *Nuestro plan de fiesta* (with Camila Fabbri) and *Rituales para la amistad* (with Daniela Rea and Elvira Liceaga). Her books have been published in nine countries and translated to English, Dutch, Italian, Portuguese, and French. This is her fourth book translated by Christina MacSweeney and published by Two Lines, including *Linea Nigra*, which was a finalist for the National Book Critics Circle's Gregg Barrios Book in Translation Prize and the National Book Critics Circle Autobiography Prize. She is editor and co-founder of Ediciones Antílope. She lives in Mexico City.

In addition to CHRISTINA MACSWEENEY's work with Jazmina Barrera, she has translated works by such authors as Elvira Navarro, Valeria Luiselli, Daniel Saldaña París, Julián Herbert, and Karla Suárez. She has also contributed to several anthologies of Latin American literature. In recent years, her translation of Jazmina Barrera's *Cross-Stitch* was shortlisted for the Queen Sofía Institute Translation Prize, Elvira Navarro's *Rabbit Island* was longlisted for a National Book Award, and Clyo Mendoza's *Fury* was a finalist for the Valle Inclán Translation Prize. In 2024, she was granted a Sundial Literary Translation Award for her translation of Verónica Gerber Bicecci's *The Company*.